"*Passionate Readers* is the perfect title for this helpful book. Pernille manages to teach us how to harness true passion in ways that will transform the readers in our classrooms. It is no small feat to take such large and lofty goals and make them tangible and real for all educators and students, and yet that is what this books offers, with heart and style to boot."

—Kate Roberts, National Literacy Consultant,
Author, and Speaker

"A good professional text is a forever resource. We go back to it time and time again for that just-right lesson or chapter we need to fuel our craft. Passion-ate Readers moves like that novel you can't put down. Tucked in between the narrative of Pernille's *five keys* and tireless risk-taking in her *passionate reading environment* are the candid voices of the kids speaking their truths, shining a light on reading identity. Make room for a new forever resource."

—Sara K. Ahmed, Literacy Coach & Consultant-in-Residence,
NIST International School, Thailand

Passionate Readers

How do we inspire students to love reading and discovery? In *Passionate Readers: The Art of Reaching and Engaging Every Child*, classroom teacher, author, and speaker Pernille Ripp reveals the five keys to creating a passionate reading environment. You'll learn how to . . .

- Use your own reading identity to create powerful reading experiences for all students;
- Empower your students and their reading experience by focusing on your physical classroom environment;
- Create and maintain an enticing, well-organized, easy-to-use classroom library;
- Build a learning community filled with choice and student ownership; and
- Guide students to further develop their own reading identity to cement them as lifelong, invested readers.

Throughout the book, Pernille opens up about her own trials and errors as a teacher and what she's learned along the way. She also shares a wide variety of practical tools that you can use in your own classroom, including a reader profile sheet, conferring sheet, classroom library letter to parents, and much more. These tools are available in the book and as eResources on our website (www.routledge.com/9781138958647)—to help you build your own classroom of passionate readers.

Pernille Ripp is a seventh grade teacher in Oregon, Wisconsin, and the creator of the Global Read Aloud (www.theglobalreadaloud.com), a literacy initiative that has connected more than 2,000,000 students since 2010 through the use of technology. She speaks internationally and writes regularly on her blog (www.pernillesripp.com). She is also author of *Passionate Learners: How to Engage and Empower Your Students*.

Passionate Readers

The Art of Reaching and Engaging Every Child

Pernille Ripp

Foreword by Donalyn Miller

Routledge
Taylor & Francis Group

NEW YORK AND LONDON

First published 2018
by Routledge
711 Third Avenue, New York, NY 10017

and by Routledge
2 Park Square, Milton Park, Abingdon, Oxon, OX14 4RN

Routledge is an imprint of the Taylor & Francis Group, an informa business

Library of Congress Cataloging-in-Publication Data
A catalog record for this book has been requested.

ISBN: 978-1-138-95863-0 (hbk)
ISBN: 978-1-138-95864-7 (pbk)
ISBN: 978-1-315-66113-1 (ebk)

Typeset in Palatino
by Apex CoVantage, LLC

Visit the eResources: www.routledge.com/9781138958647

*To the kids in room 235D, past and present; your words changed me;
don't ever let anyone tell you to stay silent.*

Contents

eResources

The appendix tools from the book are also available on our website. The material includes the following:

- Student Questionnaire—Beginning of Year
- 6-week reading habit check-in
- 25 book challenge
- Classroom library letter to parents
- Conferring sheet
- Core ELA standards
- Educator reading identity
- End of semester English survey
- End of year questionnaire
- End of year reading survey
- How are you as a reader?
- Our classroom library organization
- Reader Profile
- Self-Evaluation of Skills
- Teacher Reading Identity
- Reading Identity Challenge

To download those items, go to the book product page at www.routledge. com/9781138958647. Then click on the tab that says "Resources," and select the files. They will begin downloading to your computer.

Foreword

Donalyn Miller

I first met Pernille Ripp like many of you did: I found her on Twitter one day. I was looking for other middle school teachers to follow, and Pernille was interesting and smart. Her blog was a mix of thoughts on teaching and her cool bargain-hunting fashion finds in those days. Pernille was rooted in the technology education world at the time, and I picked up many ideas from her about blogging with my students.

In 2010, when Pernille founded Global Read Aloud, more literacy educators discovered her. She loves sharing books, but she is mindful about what books she promotes—always considering diversity and the authentic interests and needs of students. Her enthusiasm for young people and her emphasis on creating engaging learning conditions for all students inspired many of us to reach beyond the walls of our classrooms to find collaborative communities that expanded our students' understanding and awareness of the world. Through her blog, her books, and her presentations she continues to give us a glimpse into her classroom and her thinking behind her interactions with students. I consider her a colleague in the truest sense—open to ideas and willing to share her questions as much as her insights. She's a teacher's teacher, but her mindset and core beliefs always lead us back to what's best for kids.

I taught sixth grade for a decade and loved it. Mostly, I loved middle school kids. Their physical, emotional, and intellectual development is all over the place—which is endearing and maddening in turn. With one foot in childhood and one in adolescence, it's a rough time for kids. As Poppy in Holly Black's Newbery Honor book *Doll Bones* describes it, "I hate that everyone calls it growing up, but it seems like DYING." Dramatic, perhaps, but many young adolescents feel pushed into growing up when they aren't ready, while others seem to run toward their teen years at full tilt. They are figuring out who they want to be. Trying on personalities. Seeking affiliations. Asking questions about the world and their place in it. Their vitality and sense of urgency warm us like the rays of the sun. As middle school teachers, our students make our work feel vital and urgent, too.

As much as teenagers crave independence and agency, they still want adults who see them and make them feel safe. When they feel safe with you, they are all in, but it takes time to earn their trust. After spending almost half their lives to this point in school, many have become jaded. If you listen to middle schoolers, they will tell you they want to enjoy school more than they do. They want to like your class more than they do. They want to learn. They know they have a lot to learn. Instruction offering few opportunities for their self-expression and inquiry bores and frustrates them. They feel disrespected at school. Teenagers have a strong sense of justice and they rankle under rules for the sake of rules. They understand that many rules, like homework expectations and dress code policies, exist for institutional reasons that have everything to do with the sanity of adults and little to do with engaging young people in meaningful learning.

We worry so much about what kids might do that we don't let them show us what they can do.

I think the best teachers respect kids. Reading Pernille Ripp's work shows me how much respect and admiration she has for her students. She has high expectations for them, but she also sees them as people with unique needs and interests. She's a master kid-watcher and reflective practitioner—two skills vital to long-term success as a teacher. She doesn't have all of the answers, but she keeps asking smart questions about her own teaching practice. Above all, she shares some of the same qualities with her students that make this life stage so fascinating and challenging. She shares their enthusiasm and their constant disequilibrium. She shares their strength and their vulnerability.

Pernille's passion for children's learning and the value of teachers runs through every blog post she writes and every lesson she teaches. Her enthusiasm for language and its power flows from her and undoubtedly influences her students' perceptions of English class. She knows books and media, but she never lets her opinions or value systems override her students' interests and need for agency. She fiercely protects her students' rights to meaningful learning and constructs classroom activities and rituals that value her students' voices over her own. She loves our profession, but she doesn't cut teachers any slack. Even herself. She pushes us to question traditional practices that limit students' reading and writing lives while continuously reminding us of the importance of our work.

One of the qualities I most appreciate about Pernille is her reckless bravery. She takes chances. She writes incendiary things on her blog that push people. She gets on fire about things. She's upset about the state of literacy education in many classrooms, and she wants us to be upset about it, too. She knows that our students cannot wait for us to get it right. She's all in with her students, and that requires taking risks that may not pay off in the end. Better to try and fail than to teach the same way for the next thirty years and never grow. It is said that we learn as much from our mistakes as our successes (I would contend we learn more), and Pernille is not afraid to make mistakes in her teaching as long as she always keeps her students in front of her. I appreciate her willingness to challenge herself and challenge us by her example. Her humility in the face of failure and success inspires us all to try harder. She knows that she has a lot to learn. She reminds us that we all do.

Like all of us, Pernille stands on the shoulders of greatness—the influential middle school researchers and teacher leaders like John Guthrie, Ernest Morrell, Kate Roberts and Chris Lehman, Nancie Atwell, Kylene Beers, and many others who have asked important questions about adolescent literacy and learning. Throughout Pernille's interactions with her students you'll see an organic community built on a foundation of best practices steeped in decades of research, which she employs in practical, manageable ways. Reading and writing workshop meets reality. She recognizes the struggle of teaching under mandates and encourages us to look beyond them and focus on our long term literacy goals for students. Intellectual curiosity and engagement front and center, not prepackaged kits and scripted programs.

If you know Pernille's work, this book provides a deeper look at her thinking. If you're meeting her for the first time, I'm thrilled for you. Come sit in her classroom and learn with her. You'll find a dear colleague and smart mentor.

—Donalyn Miller

About the Author

Pernille Ripp is an expert in literacy and technology integration and dedicates her research and practice to developing engaged and empowered students and communities.

She is a teacher, speaker, author, blogger, and passionate advocate for education. She is a Skype Master Teacher; recipient of the 2015 WEMTA *Making IT Happen* Award; and the 2015 ISTE *Award for Innovation in Global Collaboration*. She is a proud member of the Educator Collaborative, a global think tank and professional development organization, working to innovate the ways educators learn *together*.

In 2010, Pernille founded The Global Read Aloud, a global literacy initiative that began with a simple goal in mind: one book to connect the world. From its humble beginnings, the GRA has grown to connect more than 2,000,000 students in 60 different countries.

She is the author of *Passionate Learners—How to Engage and Empower Your Students*, now in its second edition, and *Empowered Schools, Empowered Students*, both focusing on creating learning spaces and communities where students thrive and all stakeholders are empowered and passionate about learning. She has also authored *Reimagining Literacy Through Global Collaboration* published in 2016 by Solution Tree, Her work has also been featured in many print and online journals including The New York Times, *School Library Journal*, *The Guardian*, and *MiddleWeb*.

You can follow Pernille's work on *Blogging Through The Fourth Dimension*, her personal blog and a frequent *Teach100* top-rated education blog. With her mentoring, her own students' blogs have had more than 600,000 unique views since they began.

Pernille's current research interest is in creating passionate literacy environments within the restriction of our current educational systems to help students fall in love with literacy again. The door of her classroom is always open to visitors, and the students in room 235D will gladly take your questions.

Acknowledgments

I owe so much to so many; I think most of us who educate do. I owe my love of teaching to those who passed their love of curiosity and teaching onto me. I owe my love of books to the authors who write them and continue to pass them into our hands as they help us shape the world. I owe my love of learning to those that first explored the world with me—my parents and my siblings. And I owe the immense happiness I have in my life to all who are a part of it.

This book would not have been be a possibility if it wasn't for all of those educators, speakers, authors, and researchers who have paved the way for many of us. My work stands on the shoulders the likes Richard Allington; Nancie Atwell; The Two Sisters; Joan Moser and Gail Boushey; Lucy Calkins; Kylene Beers; Harvey "Smokey" Daniels; Donalyn Miller; Teri Lesene; Penny Kittle; Kelly Gallagher; Elin Keene; Kate Roberts; and Maggie Beattie Roberts and many others. You shared your knowledge with the world and unwittingly gave me the foundational knowledge needed to realize that this could be better, that teaching reading well did not have to be something that felt impossible.

This book would not have been a possibility had it not been for the challenge from my editor, Lauren Davis, who believed in me every step of the way, who did not mind my late night emails filled with self-doubt as to who I thought I was, writing a book about reading. She told me it was time to write about what we did in room 235D, so I did.

To Lin Manuel Miranda and the "Hamilton" soundtrack, to Kelly Clarkson, to Patty Griffin, and to all the other artists who were on my writing playlist when I tried to drown the noise out at coffee shops and in airplanes. Your songs are the soundtrack of this book. Can you imagine?

To Christopher Lehman, Jes Lifshitz, and Reidun Bures, whose words, friendship, and even hard truths have shaped me as an educator and pushed me to make this book more than it was. How lucky I am to consider you friends.

To all of my fellow Nerdy Book Club members: how blessed I am to have found this community that not just guides me but has also sparked so many meaningful friendships. You know who you are.

To the librarian at Bjerringbro Bibliotek who let me check out *The Clan of the Cave Bear*, even though I was clearly much too young to fully understand it. I read what I wanted to because no one ever told me I couldn't.

To the Millers: Don who took the time to tell me that I was one of the real ones, to Donalyn who took me under her wing, who cried with me when I needed it and also taught me how to fight better as she strengthened the path for more of us, to Sarah who made me remember that the future is not hopeless but instead filled with amazing young people who are changing the world already.

To the staff at Oregon Middle School and their dedication to all of the kids we teach: you epitomize what it means to work as a team and learn from each other. To my fearless principal Shannon Anderson; you have had more faith in me than I have had, thank you for seeing me as more than I thought I could be, thank you for believing in the choices we make, thank you for reminding me that our job is not just to get high test scores but to help children love learning. To all of Oregon School District: how lucky we are to work in a community that truly believes that it is always about the kids.

To my own children: Theadora, Ida, Oskar, and Augustine. One of my favorite times of the day will always be with you and a stack of books. You are the reason I do this work.

And to Brandon: the life we have built together is one I could never have imagined. Where would I be without you?

Introduction

In the Beginning: The Damage We Can Do

I read to feel lost. I read to feel what the characters feel. I read to make an amazing film or movie in my brain. I read for a purpose, I read to get better at reading and writing. I read to feel emotion and to drift off into the world of the characters. I read for all of these reasons and more.

—Patrick, seventh grader

I never meant to kill my students' love of reading; I don't think any teacher ever does. Instead, as a new teacher I followed the guidelines set forth by those who came before me and trusted in what the reading programs told me to do. I thought that if I followed these rules then my students would fall in love with reading because programs were written by experts and all experts must be as concerned with this as I was. Yet, now, I know that unless we make it our personal mission to inspire students to reengage with reading, to fall in love with text and discovery, to be open to the possibility that they may be a reader after all, then we may as well not be teaching reading. That unless we make it our mission to create passionate reading environments, then it does not matter what program we use; it will never be enough—especially when we are faced with 45-minute English language art blocks or other curricular limitations.

When Does Reading Stop Being Magical?

Starting with teaching fourth and then fifth grade, I felt the sense of urgency that comes with 9- and 10-year-olds. They somehow make you feel like a big part of their life has already passed them by, and so when students would profess to me that they hated reading, typically within the first week of school, I was always astounded. How could children so young already have resigned themselves to the fact that reading was not for them? Those years that I taught this younger age group, I saw just how important reading was to all subject areas, to all learning, whether in school or not. I knew that I was preparing students for life after school, indeed to become better human beings, yet I felt that even if I did not change their mind, someone at some point surely would. Yet, now I know that we cannot rely on the years to come. That we must take responsibility for the year that we have with our students. That we cannot stand idly by while a child declares themselves to be a non-reader and hope that someone else will figure it out. That I was wrong when I assumed that even if I did not help a child much, I did not hurt him or her either when I failed to inspire a love of reading. That surely they must have gotten something out of the year, even if what I taught did not inspire them to create a deeper reading identity or anchor the burgeoning reading identity they already had. Simply put, I hoped that other teachers would be able to do what I had not accomplished. That somehow someone with more experience would be able to help the students either reengage with reading or cement their already existing relationship. By failing to focus on creating a learning community filled with passionate readers, I see now that I was not fulfilling my job as a teacher. That in putting my faith in the teachers to come, I was giving myself a free pass to not change how reading was explored in our classroom. I just wish that I had realized it sooner.

Meeting My Biggest Challenge

Moving to middle school, to become a seventh grade English language arts teacher, only made the mission of helping students love reading more urgent. If you think fourth and fifth graders are set in their ways when it comes to their relationship with reading, wait until you meet those 12-year-olds. My everyday reality was perfectly summed up in one of my student's, Kendra, shared reading reality, "I was an average reader, who did not like reading very much. I would only read when I was forced to and I read small thin books when I had to. Also I read very slowly." Many of my students would nod in agreement with her statement and quickly share their own dark relationships with reading, while others would vehemently disagree. This is the reality we all face; we teach children who all have their own preferences and beliefs about what school should consist of. We teach children where some would prefer 45 minutes of silent reading time and are annoyed at the teacher for teaching, while others cannot wait to tell us proudly that they will never actually like reading. That reading has never been for them and that they cannot wait to be done with school so that they will never have to read another book again. When I first ventured into the world of 12- and 13-year-olds, I had no idea just how much these older students would challenge the very knowledge I brought in about reading. How much they would push my thinking as I tried to convince those who believed reading was a waste of time that they were wrong, while protecting those whose love of reading had been nourished by the teachers that came before me. This experience is, in essence, what has shaped this book; the desire to share what my students have taught me so that others may learn from our experiences. So that no one else will have to hope that the following year's teacher will finally develop or protect a love of reading.

The Added Challenge of the 45-minute English Language Art Blocks

Yet, my challenge was not just in overcoming the attitudes of teenagers, but also in managing time itself; whereas before I had had a luxurious amount of time for literacy instruction, more than 90 minutes a day, where we could revel in 30 to 40 minutes of independent reading time, I now was cut down to 45 minutes. Not just for reading, but for English language arts, where you teach reading, writing, speaking, spelling, and anything else that a child might need literacy instruction in. Forty-five minutes to somehow make a difference. Forty-five minutes to convince kids that reading was not just important but life changing. It was a daunting task and it continues to be so.

So for the past several years, it has come down to making the most of the 45-minute time frame and emphasizing the connections that my students and I have made with literacy; the 45-minute time constraint that too many teachers at the secondary level are faced with. While we pine for longer literacy blocks, we find a way to make the time that we have work for the kids that we teach. I have discovered that magic can happen within 45 minutes; it just takes more planning, more thought, and an ever-present sense of urgency. Since I do not have the luxury of more time or even a flexible schedule, we focus every minute on creating stronger bonds within our community so that students will leave knowing that they too are readers, that what we do matters, and that their contribution to the world mattered. All through the shared love of reading. All through the quest that so many of us are on.

I am so thankful for the particular challenge of 45 minutes. I am so thankful for the truths that my seventh-graders have forced me to face. I am painfully aware that not all of the truths our students speak are pretty, nor are they harmless ideas or fancy notions. That one child's resistance can lead to a whole group rebellion. That sometimes no matter the quality of teachers that came before, their access to books, or the best ideas we could have, what we are doing is still not enough. So if teaching middle school has taught me anything, it is that every day we have a chance to make a difference in the life of a child. That it truly takes a team to reach every child. That even though a 13-year-old may feel like he or she will never like reading, there is still a chance. And that the change in their perception starts with us but ends with them.

I have learned that for all of our students to have a chance of becoming the readers they were meant to be, then we must believe it more loudly than they do. At least in the beginning. That literacy and reading must mean something to matter and that we cannot just follow a program, even the best ones out there, and expect all of our students to have a successful outcome, because a great program is not enough. I thought I would last one year in seventh grade because I was not the teacher they needed, yet now as I look to the future, I see that perhaps seventh grade is where I am supposed to be. Because my students are not a lost cause in reading, just merely undiscovered at times, waiting to be listened to. To feel that their voice matters and that the identity they are trying on can still be adjusted to become that of reader. So every day I ask my students, "What are you reading?" and every day we take another step towards realizing a simple dream; a book for every child, a hope for every reader.

The Mission We Are On to Create Passionate Readers

I am a teacher who has seen that the mission we are on is one of great urgency. I am a teacher who has seen her students' test scores rise due to the changes we have implemented, but more importantly than test scores, I have seen children become readers. I am a teacher who has realized that she is not alone in this quest. I therefore stand on the shoulders of giants; the literacy greats such as Gay Ivey, Richard Allington, Lucy Calkins, Nancie Atwell, Penny Kittle, Thomas Newkirk, Kylene Beers, Gail Boushey, Joan Moser, Donalyn Miller, and others who have paved the way for me as we try to reignite the passion for reading that will help our students become better human beings, not just within our schools, but also once they leave us. That our students will not become part of the 28% that report never reading after high school, according to the Pew Research Center (Rainie and Perrin 2015), that our students will not relish the moment they no longer have to read, but instead feel a loss at the missed reading opportunities. That our students will go forth in the world and add their love of reading to that of the rest of us, so that our voices can grow louder. So while the foundation of our learning community is built on the idea of many, and I encourage you to read the books referenced throughout this volume, this book is also the story of my incredible students and how they helped me become a better teacher of reading. So this book, filled with the ideas from my students, the ideas built on the foundations set forth by literacy experts, and the ideas that I have had throughout the years as I tried to become a better teacher, will hopefully help you on your own quest as you try to reclaim the love of reading that seems to be slipping out of our schools.

There is a more powerful way to create meaningful literacy communities, there is, indeed, more we can do, because in the end, every minute matters if we really want to create passionate readers.

A Note About This Book's Structure

In each of the five keys of *Passionate Readers*, I follow a framework: What I thought and did then; what I think and do now; and suggested components of change. You will also be provided with questions to reflect upon; use these in a way that suits you best to push your own thinking and to chart your future path. This book therefore focuses in on what our five vital keys are for creating a passionate reading environment: teacher reading identity, our physical space, the classroom library, the foundations of our reading experience, and student reading identity. I believe that all five keys need to be present to have success, but also that many of us already have strengths within all of these already. This book can therefore be read from beginning to end, or read in chunks as needed as you choose what to focus on first. Use this book as you would any lesson; make it work for your needs right now as you strengthen your own practices. I hope that this setup and my honesty about my own journey to become a better reading teacher will help you on your own journey, as we join together to create meaningful reading experiences for all of the children that we get to teach.

1

Teacher Reading Identity and How It Matters

What should Mrs. Ripp tell other teachers? That she has failed butlearned from it.
—Evan, seventh grader

We were a household filled with books. I cannot remember a time when books were not in my hands, when my mother did not read aloud to us at night, or when I did not read myself to sleep under the covers, needing to finish just one more page. Growing up in Bjerringbro, Denmark, we had a beautiful public library, and I was the proud owner of a pink hand-me-down bike and my very own library card. There were no restrictions to what I checked out; the librarian merely reminded me to bring the books back. I was 10 years old when I fell in love with Jean M. Auel's *Clan of the Cave Bear*, a book that was decidedly not written for 10-year-olds. Yet I was allowed to explore her intricate world by myself, since neither my mother, nor the public librarian, ever stopped me from reading whatever I selected. Censorship was not a part of my childhood, and I became a reader because I was surrounded by reading experiences. Yet, reading is not something I connect to my school experience much. I must have read, after all; I remember the basal-like packets we had to do when we were learning to read. Yet, I do not recollect school librarians or many teachers who loved books, while I am sure they existed. I do not remember having books in our learning communities, nor having literature discussions that went past short story collections. I was not introduced to the whole-class novel until at age 13, I experienced a year of high school in Lenox, Massachusetts. Mrs. Vincent in Freshman Honors English made us read the classics and tried to get us to love them in the same way she did. Despite not having many in-school reading role models, I was a reader. Books moved across the world with me; I remember the joy I felt whenever we left America to go back home to Denmark and I was reunited with all of the books we had not been able to bring. That and the unwavering belief from my mother that I was a reader and that in our house reading mattered. I was lucky to have such a literate life, and its foundation has stayed with me through the years. I felt very connected to books as I moved into my adulthood, yet not in an outward way; instead, to me, being a reader was such an innate part of me that I did not proclaim it, nor celebrate it. Reading was connected to the very core of who I was as a person; I simply was a reader, and so I read.

Then—A Hidden Reader

Teachers can be reading role models by reading a lot of books, which might inspire their students.

—Anna, seventh grader

When I immigrated to America from Denmark at the age of 18, I marveled at the sheer availability of cheap books whenever I went to a bookstore. I no longer frequented the library as much because I could buy the books I wanted. So my shelves grew, and my stacks overflowed as I meandered from genre to genre building my very own home library. Any visitors to our house would quickly realize that books mattered, and not just adult books but picture books and favorite books from childhood, even if I mostly had them for show and not for reading. Memories were woven into the books displayed; they reminded me of where I had come from and the childhood I had. As a fourth grade teacher, though, I kept my reading life private. It was not an intentional decision to hide it, yet my reading life did not seem important. After all, I had grown up to be a reader without the "teacher as a reading role model" in my life. In hindsight, though, I know now that I did not need the teacher as a reader role model because I had it at home instead. My mother is still one of the most voracious readers I know, and she made sure that we grew up in a household that had access to many types of literature and many things to read, as well as time to read it. My childhood was filled with reading aloud and discussions of books. Not all children are as fortunate; in fact, we know from many studies that children who are raised in families who have less access to books and texts will enter school at a distinct disadvantage, already having to make up for "lost" time as they try to find success.[1] No matter how strong my literacy home was, it was not the same in school, not in any significant way. I therefore started my journey as a teacher of reading not quite sure who I needed to be other than what lesson plans told me. I was privately connected to my adult reading life but did not see how that connection should be mined to create a rich literacy life in our learning community. Because I did not read children's books or even young adult ones, I did not know what to discuss with my students beyond the few texts I had heard about from other students. I preferred adult biographies and historical novels and barely ever went into the children's section of our library or bookstore. When the latest book catalog would show up at our school, I had no idea what to pick and instead went with whatever caught my eye. When the books arrived, I did not announce them to the class but mostly placed them on the shelf, and so my selections often sat unread in our learning community, failing to interest any readers. Once in a while, I would hold them up to show them, but I did not know how to book talk them since I did not read them myself. While I identified as a passionate reader in my home life, I never made the connection between home and school. By compartmentalizing my own passion for books, I created two separate versions of me; Pernille the reader and Pernille the teacher, and neither version was enough to inspire a love of reading in others.

Yet, the idea that I needed to be a reading role model did not occur to me until I realized how many conversations we were *not* having in our learning community about reading and what it meant to be a reader. While we discussed the books we had read together through a whole-class novel or a read aloud, our conversations mostly centered on skills, such as summary and comprehension. As a class we connected, visualized, and synthesized, inspired by Ellin Keene and Susan Zimmermann's *Mosaic of Thought*, a fantastic book in its own right. Yet it never went much further than that. Reading so often felt like a checklist of strategies to get through, knowing that the end result would probably be stronger readers, but doing nothing to inspire students to read beyond the classroom. Once in a while, we would discuss favorite books, but it would be mostly in the past tense, as in our favorite picture books from childhood or books that we had enjoyed years earlier. Students rarely shared their recommendations, nor their current reads; we saved that for their six book report projects that they all had to do in a year. In short, we never really delved into what made us love these books, how we selected books, and what reading meant to us. Even though, with the luxurious gift of 90 minutes for literacy instruction, we most certainly had the time to have these conversations. Yet, they did not seem important; after all, I did not need to discuss my own reading life to continue to read, so why would students?

I was in my fourth year of teaching elementary school the day I realized that my students were disconnected from our reading community. I had started late in the year, returning from a maternity leave after having twins, and watched as a student asked my long-term substitute if he could have a pass for the school library so he could book shop. She gladly gave him one, and away he went. At the time, our classroom library filled four bookshelves and we had close to 300 books. I thought it was the model of what a classroom library should look like; 300 stand-alone titles (Neuman n.d.). The books were accessible, in neat bins, shelved by genre or author, and ready for the students whenever they needed them. Free choice in books ruled our room, and still that child was not the only one who asked for a pass. Several others gave up browsing our classroom library and instead headed for the school library. Befuddled, I asked if this happened often. "Yes, almost every day," she told me. I was confused; after all, why were they not using the books they had access to right in our classroom?

The next day, my first day back, armed with my newfound confusion, we started our standard 90-minute literacy block discussing our classroom library. Why was it underutilized? Why did they not read the books we had right here? One by one my students told me that while our library had plenty of books, they were not very good. That while they could easily check them out, they did not know how to find good books, did not know which books to read, and therefore needed someone to speak to. In their quest, they had therefore turned to our school librarian, Mr. Powers, who knew just what they should read next. A visit to him meant they came away with ideas, whereas a visit to our classroom library left them empty-handed. They knew from experience that my own list of recommendations was woefully short, and so they looked for someone else to help them. Mr. Powers would gladly hand them a stack of books and be able to book talk them all. Mr. Powers was a reader, just like them, and so they flocked to his library.

That day, filled with their truths, I knew I had a problem, and not just a classroom library one either, which will be discussed further later in this book. Instead, I had a reading role model problem, which was now leading to a reading community problem. This is not uncommon; in fact, research has suggested that when "Teachers are not knowledgeable about children's literature; they are not able to introduce students to the wealth of books available, and they may not recognize the effects of their teaching methods on students' attitude toward reading" (Short and Pierce 1990). I thought I had done what great reading teachers did; we had a library, we had choice, and we had time to read, all modeled after the teaching of the literacy books I had read. I supported students throughout my instruction and I took copious notes when we conferred. This is what successful teachers of reading did; I had, after all, done my research. Yet, those components were clearly not enough. Those components by themselves would not foster the love of reading that I had envisioned when I set out to be a teacher. There was a void that needed to be filled, and it was now up to us, as a community, to figure out what was needed to create a classroom where reading was a cornerstone of who we were as a community, and not just another class on our schedule. And I had to realize just how vital my role as a reading adult was for this change to happen. We know that having reading role models at home significantly impacts a child's success with reading in school (Lin 2003; Clark, Osborne, and Dugdale 2009), yet for some of our students this is not the reality they live in. For these children, it is even more important that we become the reading role model they may not have at home. However, I have also found that for some of my students who do, indeed, have powerful reading role models at home, this is not enough for them to become voracious readers themselves. They see those at home reading but do not always fall into the habits themselves. These children also need us to be reading role models, albeit in a different way. And so I discovered that It was not that I needed to be the best reader in the room, it was that I needed to be an example of what reading looks like after you have left school. That I needed to dedicate the same level of investment that I was asking of my students.

Consequently, on that day, four years into teaching, I realized that merely having some books and time to read them was not enough and would never inspire students to fall in love with the reading experience. Those who hated reading would never become readers who influenced others to read unless I changed the way I taught reading. Unless I changed the very reading conversation we were having. Unless I finally connected my own reading identity with that of being a reading teacher and then taught through my own love of reading rather than just following a curriculum. This therefore becomes our very first change for creating passionate readers in our learning communities; admitting or cultivating our own love of reading first. For our students to become passionate readers, we must, therefore, become visible ones ourselves.

Now—Teacher as a Reading Role Model

Teachers can be better reading role models by not acting like they have to read harder books because they're older, and instead reading books at our level so kids and teachers can connect.

—Burke, seventh grader

On the very first day of our new year together, the very first thing my new students do is to select which picture book I should read aloud for them. It never fails; my seventh graders cannot believe that they are starting with a picture book; after all, they are not little children anymore. And yet, as they vote on the one they want to hear, a familiar hush falls over the room as the students inch closer for story time. On the very first day of the new year, my students are introduced to two very large parts of my reading identity—my abundant love of picture books, as well as my firm belief that reading needs to be fun and filled with choice. Once the book is done, I wait for their reaction. They seem to always stare at me, waiting for a list of questions, but instead I ask them, "What did you think?" and their voices come to life as they react to the story. Thus the very first piece of what will become our learning community reading mosaic has been placed.

Yet, in that moment, I not only choose picture books as a way to make my own reading identity a focal point, but also to offer it up as a way to start our reading conversations. By offering a small glimpse into what I love as a reader, it in turn sets the stage for students to contemplate what they love. It allows them to start questioning what they think a middle school English class will feel like, because most students certainly are not expecting picture books. In fact, as Emily wrote, "I think teachers should use picture books with kids because we normally are told to read chapter books, yet as a seventh grader you get kind of bored reading books with no pictures and you miss being a kid." By 12 years old, some of my students miss being a child . . . so part of my mission is to remind them of the original love they felt for reading when they first discovered it. Thus knowing myself and how I developed as a reader, intentionally drives the instruction as students start to explore their own identities; this exploration becomes part of our foundation as a passionate reading community. For me, this student-focused and -driven exploration is vital because the learning community is not about us as educators, it is about the very students we teach.

So as you think of your own reading identity, what comes to mind? What great experiences have you had with reading? What are the not so great ones? How have you developed as an adult reader versus how you identified as a child learning to read? These are all things that we should reflect on as we decide what type of reading environment and, indeed, experience, we would like to create for our students. Because whether we know it or not, these are the very things that drive us forward in our instruction, and so if we are not aware of our biases then we will have no way of controlling them when we teach. Whatever we choose to *not love* in our reading instruction is not given much attention by the students. While we may follow lesson plans, we ultimately decide how we will teach something, and students are masters at recognizing when we, as teachers, are merely going through the motions. That means that how we feel about reading will directly influence how all of the students we teach also feel about reading. As a middle school teacher, I take that notion incredibly seriously; after all, I teach more than 130 students. If I do not love reading and proclaim it loudly, then what will become of all of those students? Simply put, we must be readers ourselves, if we are to instill a love of reading. Like Kaylee says, "Teachers should show us how much they enjoy reading to help us love reading more."

Questions to ponder as you consider your own reading identity (by no means an exhaustive list):

◆ Are you a reader? If yes, why? If no, why not?
◆ What types of books do you reach for when you are relaxing?
◆ What types of books do you abandon?
◆ How quickly do you abandon a book?
◆ How do you share what you have read with others?
◆ Whom do you share it with?
◆ What would you like to do when you have finished a book?
◆ How do you do in book discussions?
◆ What are your book gaps, meaning what do you not read?
◆ Would you consider yourself a bad, average, or good reader?
◆ What type of reading experience would you like your students to have?

Within our own exploration of reading identity, we should uncover cornerstones to build our learning community reading environment on. Within our own experiences as a reader, we can start to consider the identities that our students bring with them. What are things that propelled us toward books or further away from them? How do we react in our adult lives when given reading tasks such as summarizing, analysis, or discussion? Most adults do not like to create a project—a written report, summary, or craft—after finishing their book, and yet how often have we asked students to do this very thing? The same thing goes for abandoning books. How often do we leave books in our wake simply because they failed to catch our interest, yet expect our students to read a certain number of pages, or never abandon a book because we told them so? Realizing that we carry our own innate biases when it comes to reading is an important step in cultivating our reading identity. We have so much influence on the type of reading environment we create, even when faced with a set curriculum or constricted by time, so knowing how that shapes the small decisions we make is vital for how we end up changing our way of teaching.

Sometimes it is our very adulthood that gets in the way of us creating passionate reading environments. Sometimes the very things that we hold dear as adult readers are the first things we remove from our learning communities. In fact, some reading teachers report never reading themselves, yet this is one large thing in our control that research shows will make a difference in creating stronger reading environments (Collins, Cremin, Mottram, Powell, and Safford). This is not the only thing that will make a difference to our students, but it is a major one. So as you reflect on your own reading identity, I encourage you to look at yourself through a critical lens. What are your fundamental beliefs about reading and how are these impacting students? One way to do this is to take the Teacher Reading Identity survey in the appendix and then change the very things that may be standing in your own way or strengthening the things that already are in place.

Component of Change: Strategies to Infuse Your Own Reading Identity Into Your Learning Community

Teachers should not be afraid to make changes.
—Noah, seventh grader

There are many ways that our teacher reading identity can be infused into our learning community or school without it becoming the focal point. When we decide to bring our own identity as readers into our learning communities, conversations about what it means to be a reader occur naturally if we allow them to. These become examples for our students of what adult reading role models look like and should inspire further conversations as their own reading lives take shape. Here are a few key pieces that may help you bring your own reading identity in.

Strategy One—Make Reading Visible Throughout Your Environment

Making my reading visible is one of many ideas I have gained from educator and blogger Jillian Heise. In her blog post "Celebrating a Culture of Literacy Displays" (Heise 2013) she writes,

> One of the things I have really worked on this year is spreading and sharing my love of reading by creating a culture of literacy throughout the school and sharing my reading life with students beyond the walls of my learning community.

In her post, she shares the ideas of how she models her own life as a reader not only to her students, but to anyone who happens to pass by her learning community. Much like Jillian, I have a "Just Read" display outside of our learning community door. Students can see which book I have just finished, how many books I have read so far this year, and a rating of a book as well. This is something every teacher of reading should do; in fact, it should be present for all staff members at a school. As Donalyn Miller writes in *Reading in the Wild*, "When we promote books to children and share our reading lives with them, we offer more than another great book recommendation or reading cheerleader; we invite them into a society that reveres reading and readers" (2013, 91). Making our reading visible through posters, displays, and even book challenges is a sure way to show students that we are readers in both word and action. That reading is something we give importance to and

Image 1.1 How many books has Mrs. Ripp read?

also something that we see as an integral part of who we are. The opposite is true as well; if reading is merely something we teach, and not something we live, then why should students take us seriously when we tell them how important reading is to future success?

So in our school, many staff members showcase their reading, and not just those that teach reading, but anyone who reads. I love that reading is visible throughout our building and that the love comes from many. Our administrators proudly book talk books to those that want to hear it, and our beautiful library lies at the very center of the building. Helping students, and sometimes other staff members, fall in love with reading is not just something that we speak about; we live it as a communal mission and try to keep the reading conversation alive.

Ideas to Try—Inspired by Members of the Nerdy Book Club

- ◆ Create "Just Read" pictures for all staff members and encourage staff to share their reading lives.
- ◆ Create favorite book displays throughout the school or decorate doors or book covers.
- ◆ Showcase book recommendations on announcements.
- ◆ Invite other staff members in to recommend books to your class.
- ◆ Incorporate a communal reading time.
- ◆ Set up book swap trees throughout the school for students to grab books to read and take home.
- ◆ Have picture books in the lunch room to inspire more reading.
- ◆ Create book baskets for school buses, so older students can read to younger students.
- ◆ Purchase and install a Little Free Library outside of your school.

Strategy Two—Set Public Reading Goals

Much like I ask my students to set a 25 book goal or higher, inspired by the 40 Book Challenge from Donalyn Miller in *The Book Whisperer*, I set one for myself and publicly check in with my students on it. My goal is not for quantity only, but also for change of habit. I read too fast, which leads to a lack of comprehension, abysmally made clear when I cannot remember characters' names or authors of books I like. Changing my reading pace therefore has been a public goal of mine for several years. Education as a whole seems to have been obsessed with reading speed for a while now, often tying in reading comprehension scores with how quickly a child can answer a question, and so admitting that my too-fast reading speed is a problem sends a powerful message to those students who have been told that they are slow readers. As Thomas Newkirk writes, in his article "Reading Is Not a Race" (2012),

By slowing down, by refusing to see reading as a form of consumption or efficient productivity, we can attend to word meanings and sound, building a bridge to the oral traditions that writing arose out of. We can hold passages in memory, we can come to the view that good texts are inexhaustible. And by being patient and deliberate, we can tackle difficult texts.

So I speak publicly about my failures to comprehend and my goal to slow down. I speak publicly to the number of books I would like to enjoy, setting a high but attainable goal that I can track with my students. Students are asked to set their own goals as well, emphasizing that they should be challenging themselves. In elementary school, their minimum goal was 40 books, much like Miller's, yet in middle school it has been adjusted to 25 books, since I cannot offer them more than 10 minutes of independent reading time in class. (See the appendix for details of our 25 Book Challenge) If I were to say 40 books, some students would give up before even trying. For some reason, 25 is not as scary a number, yet it spurs many into reading action. As Ryan wrote,

Image 1.2 My "Just Finished Reading" Poster

I think I am reading more because of the 25 book challenge. 25 seemed like a big number at the beginning of the year but now I have almost read 25 books and I am still going to read even more because I enjoy it.

Publicly setting goals with students and then performing the same check-in as they are expected to means that my students see what adult reflection can look like and also gives them an opportunity to know that teachers are not perfect. Students setting reading goals is widely recognized as boosting their reading achievement (Parrish n.d.), so it only makes sense that we set goals alongside them. Some of my students choose to compete against me in their own reading goals, which is fine; however, competition is generally not a part of our learning community as it usually only ends up benefitting those who know they will do well.

Ideas to Try:

- As students reflect and set goals for each quarter or other predetermined set of time, reflect and set your own goals. I love the reading goal sheets that Jennifer Serravallo has created in her *The Reading Strategies Book* (2015) and have tweaked it only slightly to fit our needs. However, this sheet can be overwhelming for some, so I always encourage teachers to discuss what types of goals are most meaningful for their students and their instruction. Sometimes a student's goal is simply to read more often, rather than a deeper skill goal.
- Share your own goals with the students; you can even create a poster to remind yourself or some other public display of what you are working on.
- When students reflect on their own progress, reflect on your own. What needs to be focused on more? What else do you need to work on?
- Bring up your progress and achievement or failure when teaching; this signals to students that this is a living, breathing goal, and not one that you set and then promptly forgot all about.

Strategy Three—Confronting Our Bad Habits

One winter, faced with mounting work, I fell into the longest reading slump I have had in years. Books were tossed aside after only a few pages and replaced with the shiny games on my iPad. When guilt finally forced me to stick with a book, I skimmed pages and raced through it to finish. I selected books based on how short they were so I could tell my students I at least read something. Whereas in the past I would have hidden these terrible habits from my students, I instead embraced them and then decided to come clean in the learning community. Discussing our bad habits as readers is a powerful conversation starter for students. It directly indicates that we are not perfect reading adults. That even though we value reading, we sometimes do not read. That even the most passionate readers can fall into bad habits, but what matters is how we combat them. How we build awareness and how we un-slump ourselves when we recognize what is happening to our reading lives. How often do we tell our students to be honest with us, yet then hide our own not-so-perfect ways from them? These conversations have created a stronger sense of a connected reading community; after all, when one person decides to share his or her reading truths, it often inspires others to share as well.

Ideas to Try:

- Honestly reflect; what bad habits do you carry as a reader?
- Share your bad habits as you teach reading strategies or other lessons. This is not to dominate the conversation, but instead to share what an actual reading adult goes through.
- Confront assumptions about "strong" readers head on. What do students think that strong readers do? Many think that strong readers always know what to read, can always find the time, and never feel like not reading, but we know that this is not always true.
- Keep a reading journal of some sort to see when you read best and when you read the most. What keeps you in the habit of reading? What stops you from reading?

Strategy Four—Share Your Reading Plans

Much like we ask students to set reading plans throughout the year, we must also set our own. Discuss your own to-be-read list; share your book piles and your excitement over the next installment of a series or the dread of a beloved series coming to an end. Share when you plan on reading and also how you find time to read every day or however often you read. Show students that reading is not something that just magically happens but instead is something you plan for, that way they can see what habits need to be in place to become a successful reader. Some students think that reading will just happen by an external force and do not see the role their own decisions make in their lack of reading. Showcasing the thought that goes into a successful daily reading experience is therefore a must in order to highlight more unknown parts of what it means to be a reader. While the point of these conversations in the beginning will be to showcase yourself as a reading role model, as the year progresses it should morph into a conversation starter for the students to share their own reading plans. We do not want to create learning communities that center on the teacher as the only role model, but instead facilitate conversation and community that centers around all of the members of it being reading role models for each other. Our sharing should lead to more student sharing, so when you do share make sure there is time for students to share about their reading plans as well. As the year progresses, emphasize the focus on students speaking about their reading plans, rather than your own. After all, the journey you are supporting in your learning community is not meant to only boost your own reading identity, but more importantly that of your students.

Ideas to try:

◆ When you ask students to write down titles of books read, write your own down with them. Students see my finished books on Instagram through a common hashtag, or I even update a reader's notebook in front of students under the document camera.
◆ Ask what their reading plans are and be specific; where will they read, for how long, what will they read? Then share your own specific plans.
◆ Through a book talk on Monday, discuss the reading you did over the weekend and evaluate yourself. Did you really get as much reading done as you wanted? Do not strive for perfection but instead for honesty.

Strategy Five—Discover and Then Explore Your Own Reading Gaps

On the last Sunday of every month, you can find a lively reading conversation happening on Twitter through the use of the hashtag #Titletalk. Co-founded by Colby Sharp, an extraordinary third grade teacher in Parma, Michigan, and the Book Whisperer herself, educator and author Donalyn Miller, it was through this chat that I first became aware of my own reading gaps; the books that I tend to stay clear of simply because they are of a certain genre or deal with a certain topic. Through this chat, I discovered that my book gaps include dog books, mermaid books, and most sports-related books as well. Rather than give books that fell within these categories a proper chance, I instead dismissed them outright, not investing the money to place them in our library, or if one snuck in, I would never book talk it.

While this may not seem like a big deal to most teachers who read, I have realized over the years just how much our book gaps, and therefore book preferences, influence the reading lives of our students. When we do not book talk certain types of books, let alone purchase them, then we are in turn passing our book gaps onto our students. We are subliminally showing students that there are entire genres that are not worthy of our attention. And it happens to all of us. Therefore, recognizing your own book gaps means that you can do something about it. So take a critical look at your library and this time do not just look at what you have, but instead look at what you are missing. Which books do you not purchase? Which books do you not read? Which books do you not book talk? Then discuss that newfound knowledge with students so that they can reflect on their own reading gaps. My students will book talk books to me based on my known reading gaps because they want to persuade me to tackle the gaps head on. I am so grateful for their recommendations.

Ideas to try:

◆ Evaluate your own reading life; which genres or formats do you stay away from?
◆ Discuss your book gaps with students. What has led you to them? Why do you need to change your opinion? How can they help you find great books that will change your mind?
◆ Challenge yourself to read at least one book from each of your book gaps; ask your students for recommendations.
◆ Book talk at least one book from each of your book gaps once a month.
◆ Ask your students which types of book topics they would like more of in your library; then do your best and add these suggestions to the class.

Strategy Six—Critically Evaluate Your Own Reading

While reading has always been a part of my life, my husband considers himself a limited reader. Growing up working class meant that free time was for work to help the family, not leisure activities like reading, and so books and the discovery of them were not of importance. He grew up to be a functioning, intelligent, empathetic adult who does not read many books, and until he met me, he was just fine with that. He is not alone—there are many adults, 28% as referenced earlier, that have not read a book in the last 12 months. I cannot help but wonder how many of them are teachers, and that scares me. When we urge students to do something, we must do it ourselves. My students have told me for years that all teachers should try their own homework, and they have also told me how they wish their teachers understood what it feels like to be a student in today's classroom. So when we expect our students to read every day, both in class and out; when we expect them to be ready to discuss their reading experiences; when we teach them how to be successful readers, but we do not read for pleasure ourselves, then our actions, unfortunately, will always speak louder than our words. Students can smell a fraud from miles away and will have no problem not reading, if you don't. So if reading is not a part of your life right now, consider this the biggest gift you can give yourself; find a book, find a quiet moment, and open its pages. Make it a book that you can recommend to students, that you can personally hand to leave as "a child" and tell them that you thought of them as you read it. Develop your own reading habits alongside your students, and be honest with them; why are you not reading? What does not appeal to you about books? Go through the same experiences that you create for your students so that you can pull from those experiences as you help them shape their identity. Take it one book at a time, but make it an urgent to-do. Discover your own passion for reading so that you can pass it on to your students as well, just like Anika wrote when asked what advice she would give teachers who teach reading, "Read kids' books yourself, that way if you read a good kids' book you can help them find a good book."

Ideas to try:

- ◆ Be honest! How much reading do you really do every day? If it is less than 20 minutes, you should probably expand upon it.
- ◆ Start your own to-be-read stack or list. Always have a book handy when you finish a book so you do not fall into a reading slump.
- ◆ Follow the advice you give to students for creating rich reading lives. See what advice does not work and adjust accordingly.
- ◆ Expand on the time you spend reading books for children; every single book you read is a book talk waiting to happen.

There are other facets to our reading identity that can become conversation starters in our learning communities, but we must uncover these purposefully. What else can you bring into the learning community to show students what it means to be an adult reader? Who else can you tap into in your education community? I am surrounded by colleagues who read, and not just the teachers who teach components of literacy, and I am grateful every single time another adult in our building speaks to children about their reading life. Too often, we feel like we are the sole crusaders, yet we forget that we are often in buildings surrounded by people who also love reading, even if their instruction does not mirror our own. This is clear to me in middle school where there may only be a handful of English-related teachers, but a whole community of teachers that also read. So find your allies and spread the passion. Make reading a focal point of your community, expanding it beyond your school if possible. What matters is that we are in tune with what we see ourselves as so that we can help students begin their own exploration and chart a path for how they will grow in the time we may have with them. For great ideas of how to spread a joy of reading, I was inspired by both *Reading in the Wild* by Donalyn Miller and Susan Kelley and *Book Love* by Penny Kittle. Both are excellent resources for further reading on how to spread a passion for reading.

A word of caution, though, as this chapter comes to an end; sometimes we can go too far in trying to influence student reading lives. Our reading journeys can become the roadmap for how others' reading journeys should look and feel like, often with devastating results; students who leave our rooms more frustrated with reading than they were when they came in. This has happened to me as I held students' to the same exacting standards I hold my own reading to; frustrated children who moved further away from reading than before they entered our learning community. So as you consider your own reading life, make sure you are not trying to mold that of your students into a replica of yours. Make sure that you speak of the different ways to be a reader and not just the one way. Make sure that your face does not condemn a child's reading choices just because it is not to your liking. Make sure that your classroom library has books for all students and not just books that you would like to read. Make sure that students can comfortably read in their environment and not just based on how you would like to read. Make sure that all children's unique journey is the focal point of the path they are on to become passionate readers, and not the artificial path you have created for them.

While the teacher's reading identity should never be the drive behind our passionate reading communities, it can start off as a knot to bind us all together. When we, as adults, share our true selves, bad habits and all, we are signaling to students that this is a safe environment for them to also share their true selves. That in this space, we will not judge nor condemn their reading habits but instead explore and strengthen them. We must showcase our own imperfections so that students can feel comfortable sharing their own. We must remember that while our students are on a reading journey, it is not our reading journey they are on. They instead need to be taught the tools of how to navigate to become successful readers while they are with us, but also successful readers as they leave us, because we cannot create environments that are centered around us; they must be centered around students. As Donalyn Miller writes in *Reading in the Wild*, "If we really want our students to become wild readers, independent of our support and oversight, sometimes the best thing we can do is get out of the way" (109). Part of being a teacher of reading is therefore knowing when to get out of the way of all individual children so they can forge their own connections to reading, because it is the connection that will sustain them as they leave our learning communities. It is their burgeoning belief that they can become or remain children who read that will spur them to keep trying. But they will not believe us if they do not see us a reading adults.

Questions to ponder as you weave your own reading identity into your learning community:

- ◆ When did your reading journey begin?
- ◆ What reading memories influence you now?
- ◆ What do your students know about your reading life?
- ◆ What are your book gaps and what can you do to change them?
- ◆ Who are your reading allies?
- ◆ How can you weave your own reading life more into your own instruction?
- ◆ How will you make a (re-)commitment to your reading life?

Note

1 http://teacher.scholastic.com/products/face/pdf/research-compendium/access-to-books.pdf

2

How Our Physical Space Affects
Our Reading Experiences

A classroom should look welcoming and cozy, not a room thatis dull
or empty, but a room with character and tons of good books all over.
—Averi, seventh grader

I was 28 when I was hired for my first classroom position. As an eager new teacher, I spent weeks setting up my new learning community, making it just so for the 8- or 9-year-olds that would be my very first class. Tables were moved around until the classroom flow felt right, supplies were placed in high-traffic areas, and I laminated almost everything that I used. My newly purchased label maker ran out of tape as I meticulously labeled everything, claiming my teacher territory one label at a time. One poster detailing classroom routines, such as when to sharpen a pencil or how to get supplies, was remade twice and hung prominently in the learning community. Organizing and setting up was my way of dealing with the first-day nerves that still affect me to this day. Yet, in my eagerness to prepare, I missed a vital component in my preparation; how the overall feel of the classroom would shape the reading experience the students would have. Instead, I focused on finding the perfect spot for desks, knowing that this is where they most likely would remain for the year, as well as finding the perfect way to situate chairs. Flow mattered, but mostly because I needed to be able to circulate efficiently as I taught. As I wrote in my book *Passionate Learners*, "I was so wrapped up in managing my space that I lost focus on what was important in the space; the students" (30).

While my classroom looked much like many other learning communities one might encounter, it did not feel welcoming to the core. It felt functional, efficient, and workable, all great components of a classroom but not its most important ones. We were a learning community where much instruction took place, including reading and writing, but not a learning community defined by its reading experience, not like we are today. Now when students enter our classroom they marvel at the books, the choice in seating, the lighting, and even just the feel of the room. Many of my students tell me that the room feels calm and safe. The students enter and know that in this room they have choice, they have voice, and that reading matters above all, not *my* reading, but *their* reading and the reading they hope to experience. With every choice we make in our learning communities, we should be looking at the whole experience it creates, not just whether it works in the short-term quest to make our rooms work.

Then—A Learning Community With Books as an Accessory to Learning

Teachers should always have classroom libraries because it makes the room look welcoming, with stories from people from around the world right in your reach.

—Parker, seventh grader

For someone who has grown up in libraries and a home filled with books, who comes from the land of "Hygge," a Danish term that is not just a verb but also a noun that describes the togetherness we try to create in our environments, I had missed the opportunity to create momentum when it came to our learning community. Not just in our classroom library—where no books faced out, no books were highlighted, and beside the alphabetization there was no sorting or grouping of books—but also in the space itself. While I certainly had attempted to create an inviting learning community, after all which teacher doesn't, I had forgotten what it would mean to be a student in that very space. I had taken to heart the word of experts who told me students craved routines and predictability and who left nothing to chance (Wong and Wong n.d.). Yet in this endeavor to create a learning community that experts would be proud of, that parents would marvel at, and that others would deem to be efficient based upon looks alone, I forgot to leave room for the very children I taught. In my beautiful bulletin boards, labeled shelves, and just-right table groupings, there simply was little opportunity for the students to leave their mark. And it showed. Students visited rather than lived in the room throughout my first years of teaching. They had their spaces, sure, but everything that would have allowed them to feel like the room also belonged to them was controlled by me. They were not allowed to say what would go on display on our bulletin boards; in fact, they were not even allowed to say whether they wanted their work displayed or not. They did not share the control of our library, our seating arrangements, or even projects that we did. The formality of our room, even if it looked colorful and inviting, was something that immersed itself throughout our day, and particularly in our literacy program. Students had little voice when it came to what they did in literacy, and so they certainly also had little voice when it came to how our environment looked and felt. Our room was functional, leading to just fine teaching, but certainly not inspiring most students to think about who they were as readers, as learners, or as human beings.

Yet before I denigrate my new teacher self too much, something good did come of those few years where I had little idea what I was doing; a profound sense of knowing that this could be done in a better way. That teaching anything, let alone reading, was not meant to be a checklist type of teaching. That it had to extend beyond what we were supposed to do when we followed whatever program we were told to follow, and instead became something bigger than that. An endeavor that would revolve around creating opportunities for students not just to grow as readers as measured by a test scores, but to grow as readers. Because my students did grow as readers those first few years, at least according to their test scores they did, but they did not change much. They did not leave with memories tied into favorite books we had shared or reading experiences we had created. They left ready to read if they already liked reading or ready to not read if they did not. So I knew that when I started to change the way I taught reading, I had to look at the very environment we had our literacy experiences in and start there. I had to evaluate the environment, knowing that I had no budget to change it, but still had to find a way to create a significant change in order to signal a different type of experience ahead for all of those students I would be lucky enough to teach. And that change turned out to be found in the small details rather than in the big furniture pieces that dominated our environment.

Now—An Adaptive Literacy Environment That Works

A warm, cozy place will make kids feel more welcome. A few pillows, some comfortable chairs or bean bags will interest students in having a good book to read. A class library will be an excellent choice because then one good book and a comfy seat will inspire them to read.

—Emma H., seventh grader

If you were to enter our learning community, Room 235D at Oregon Middle School, Oregon, Wisconsin, you might be surprised. After all, there is really nothing fancy about it. You might be surprised at the sheer number of books. At the sheer number of picture books. At the familiarity of the furniture we all seem to have a version of—wooden desks and tables, plastic-backed chairs. Our learning community, for I share it with my students, is really nothing spectacular to look at. While we do have a wonderful window that provides us with light, our room will probably never be featured as an example of what a beautiful classroom looks like. And yet, if you were to enter it while students are present, perhaps a few weeks into the school year, I hope you would feel what I feel every day—this quiet sense of belonging, of safety, of pride, of courage, of creativity, and even of empowerment. As one student said on our first quarter survey, "I would not change how calm the room feels." Every year I have asked my students what they would like to change about our environment, and so far the most prevalent response has been— nothing. It is fine the way it is. While we may dream of a coffee shop, or perhaps more room, more yoga balls, or even a couch, my students seem to think that it works for us, and I would have to agree. The feel of our learning community is what I hope all children will feel when they enter our schools: welcome, safe, belonging. The feel of our learning community is part of the

Image 2.1 Our classroom waiting for students to fill it

foundation for creating a passionate reading environment, one that connects us to each other and the world, and so it is something we must pursue and not just leave up to chance.

With the push for flexible seating and other emphasis on our classroom environments, I worry that we once again as an education community are throwing money at a bigger problem, student engagement, without actually thinking about its root cause. Students become disengaged for many reasons, but our furniture choice is typically not one of them. Instead, it is how we use our furniture that can lead students to feel like in our classrooms, in our schools, they do not matter. This was no more apparent to me than a few years ago after I had spoken at length about "our classroom," and a fifth grade student raised his hand and said, "How can you say this is our classroom, when it says 'Welcome to Mrs. Ripp's Room' above our door?" The next day the sign came down. For too long we have spent an awful lot of time thinking about the setup of our learning community, whether it be in the days leading up to a new school year or even every morning. We move furniture the way we see fit, without asking students to partake in this seemingly minor component of our day. While many learning communities no longer employ the traditional rows facing the teacher, there still is a distinct formality to many classroom setups. There still is a very clear power structure in place made apparent by who arranged the desks and who decided the seating. Therefore, within our furniture arrangements, we communicate some subtle, or perhaps not so subtle, messages to students. How we place our desks and chairs tell students what type of lesson to expect, whether they will be a part of a discussion or silent work, whether they will sit with friends or with strangers. When we tell students that they are not allowed to move the furniture around, we remove the opportunity for them to figure out how the physical space impacts their learning and their decision-making. When we remove even the simplest of choices, such as where to work in a space, we are effectively telling children that we do not trust them to make good decisions, whether they have proved this to us or not. No wonder our students can come to us seemingly disengaged as they enter our classrooms; think of the messages the very structure and space of our learning environment may be communicating to them.

So our space now functions on a couple of common expectations:

◆ Find a place to work that works for you and for those who surround you.
◆ Find a chair or something to sit on if needed that works for you. (Students can select from yoga balls, regular plastic chairs, or regular chairs with exercise bands across their bottom legs as a way to fidget

with their feet. Some also choose to borrow my office chair, sit on the floor, or sit on outdoor chairs in the back of the room.)

◆ How you work is often up to you. (Students are asked to use their time wisely, to embrace the quiet when we read, but to speak as we learn.)

◆ Ideas are always welcome and often embraced, and while we have routines, we are not afraid to change them as we see fit.

Children choose where they sit and whom they work with; if they make poor choices, we handle it on a case-by-case basis. While most of my classes in the past seven years have been able to handle the responsibility of having no teacher-mandated seating charts, there have been exceptions. Often a few children cannot handle the responsibility of choice just yet, even after they have been given multiple chances, and so a seating chart is instated for a short time. To ensure that this arrangement does not impede those who can handle the responsibility, I ask all students to list the names of those they would like to sit by and then try to accommodate almost all requests. The few kids who cannot choose wisely are placed throughout the learning community to work. We try this for a few weeks and then try no seating arrangement again and repeat the process as necessary. Often all children can make better choices once they have worked successfully within the learning community.

Books surround us in all of their forms and are a constant companion as we learn. We are a living, breathing learning community it seems, swathed in blue light from our covered fluorescent light bulbs and immersed in reading. We are a mini library meant to be explored, a space where all children are accepted and welcomed. We are nothing fancy when it comes to how we look, but we are a community of readers, even if some are not sure they belong there yet.

Component of Change: Changing Your Learning Space to Support Your Vision

How should a classroom look to make you want to read in it? Like Mrs. Ripp's . . .

—Austin, seventh grader

What I have come to realize after a few years of purposefully trying to create a learning environment where students feel welcome is that it is not about the furniture we have, it is about the experiences we create. As I wrote in *Passionate Learners*, "It is not how your learning community looks, it is how it feels . . ." (29). It is about how we try to create learning communities where students are not pushed into a deficit mindset from the moment they enter. One where students do not feel powerless, but instead feel like they have control over many parts of their learning day. The literacy experiences we hope to have deserve to happen in a learning community where students can feel like their whole self is accepted and that there is room for them. When we, as the teachers, overtake a space, determined to make it fit us like we would our home, we make little room for the very students we teach and their lives. They feel like visitors rather than as members of a communal space that is ever changing to fit their needs and yours. So as educators we must strike a balance between creating a functional learning community that shows off our personality and one that welcomes all students. As you evaluate your space, do not worry about the things you lack: I think we all would love better furniture, better rooms, better insert whatever thing here. Instead, focus on what you have. Take a step back and try to look through the eyes of your students; how would they describe the learning environment to other students? Better yet, ask them, because it is within their truths that we can find our inspiration to change the space we function within. This can be done through a brief survey or even a short conversation. In fact, almost all of my changes in our classroom have come because of student requests. This is why we have yoga balls for those who prefer to bounce a little, but also why we still have regular chairs for those who would find a ball to be a distraction. This is why I embrace the individual desks we still have, so that the students can configure them the way they see fit, as well as the whiteboard paper-covered tables where students choose to sit. This is why our library is our main focus in the learning community, not the teacher's space or the whiteboard.

While many of us dream of bigger and more functional classrooms, many of us also know that in this time of budget crunches, our furniture and the space itself is usually not a priority. Yet, facing this reality should not make us feel hopeless but instead should allow us greater creativity. How can we create passionate reading communities with what we have? How can we create an inviting space for all without a budget to fuel our design changes? How can we create a space where students feel they are connected to their own reading exploration, as well as that of their peers? Now, a disclaimer; I am not a crafty person, nor do I like to decorate my learning community. For many years I have asked students to take over any bulletin boards or decorations as a whole—they always do a better job than I. I have also moved away from overly "feminine" rooms inspired by Pinterest, not because there is anything inherently wrong with them, but because I worry that it immediately makes some of our students distance themselves from us. Not all students like to be surrounded by chevron, pastel colors, or even polka dots (or vice versa). Do our learning communities allow everyone to feel at home?

Here are a few things to reflect upon or ask your students. This is by no means an exhaustive list but a place to start.

Do You Have Furniture That Is Not Needed, That Serves Little Purpose?

While it is hard to give up furniture, I have tried to pare down as much as I can over the years. As every piece has left our classroom, hopefully to be utilized better elsewhere, the change has been significant; more room for movement, more breathing space. This includes when I said goodbye to my teacher desk, a move I made more than seven years ago, and instead replaced it with a small table in the back corner. Ridding myself of such a major piece of furniture not only freed up space, but it changed the whole feel of the room for me; no longer did I feel as the teacher as ruler, but reassigned my role to be one that was more with the students rather than behind a desk. I continue to try to purge every year when I can, which can be hard when you teach larger class sizes, and yet I pay attention to what is used in our learning community and then try to figure out how furniture can serve dual purposes whenever possible. This is why one triangular table in the corner of our room is not just where all of the supplies are; it also holds their assignment bins and all of the carpet squares, as well as having the recycling bin underneath. This is why I have been able to get rid of most of our individual desks, trading them in for trapezoid group tables instead to free up more space in the room. If you are unsure whether you can get rid of something, try it out for a few days by removing it to somewhere else. If your learning community still functions, then give it up for good, if not, then bring it back.

What Message Does the Furniture Setup Send to Those Who Enter the Room?

Chances are that if you saw our classroom in the morning and then came back at the end of the day, furniture would have been moved, certainly all of the chairs have. On the very first day of school, I tell students that this is their space and so they should manipulate the furniture as they see fit. Inevitably they forget, so I remind them throughout the year; use it how you see fit so that you can learn best. We all know just how much influence our environment will have on our moods, so it is vital for students to be able to manipulate the room into a working space for them. We discuss common-sense guidelines: no exclusions of others, room is needed so people can move, and make sure it boosts your learning, not hinders it, but inevitably the students experiment throughout the year, figuring out what their unique configurations should be. I have purposefully declined heavy tables so that my students can always easily move the tables around as needed. Same things goes for the chairs we

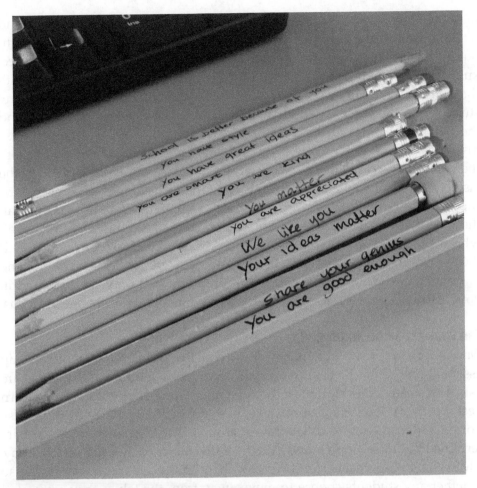

Image 2.2 Affirmation in small places

use, and anything else movable in the learning community. Most people do not notice the teacher's table in the corner, nor should they. I am rarely there unless there are no students in the room. So glance around your own room—what message does it send to those who use it? Where does the learning take place and where is information centered?

According to the Layout of the Room, What Is Most Important?
I always get a little self-aware whenever visitors enter our classroom; what will they think about how plain it is? In fact, when the students are not in the room, our room looks pretty bare; functional, but not very alive, perhaps a little like a library sleeping at night. Yet for anyone who enters, I know that they will see right away what matters in our room—reading. You simply cannot miss the shelves of books coupled with the book displays. You cannot

miss the "Just read" poster display I keep next to our front door. Books and reading are everywhere; within reach, within grasp at all times. Throughout my years, I have allowed books to slowly take up more and more space, knowing that the books we have in our learning community, coupled with those in our school library, are what will make the biggest difference to many students. So the students laugh as they see the bookshelves get added and they tell me that one day we will run out of space, but I would rather immerse my students in a book flood every day knowing how much it will benefit them in the long run (Elley and Mangubhai 2016). As one child told me on the last day of school one year, "You know what made the biggest difference, Mrs. Ripp? All of the books just waiting for me to grab them." And he was right, all those books do make the biggest difference. So look through a visitor's eyes; what would they think was most important in your classroom or school if they entered? What ideas about you would they walk away with after being in your space? What message is being communicated on your walls and in your learning spaces? If it is not the message you hoped for, change the focus.

Can Students Gather Naturally?

On the very first day of school, we do several group collaborative projects, an essential one being the creation of our classroom expectations. Students are asked to create a description of the type of learning environment they learn best in, what it feels like, sounds like, and looks like, and they discuss these norms within their first collaborative groups. These groups are not predetermined but instead are based on where the students choose to sit that day. I watch and observe as I try to see how their group dynamics work and also whether any students choose to move away from the tables they are seated at. Seeing how students start to use the space and its furniture is a large indicator to me as to what needs to change. Can the students move around? Are they squeezing in anywhere? Is a table placement not working? These are all thoughts that go through my mind as they work together for the very first time. After we have discussed our expectations, I tell the students that the room is theirs to manipulate. That the furniture is almost all moveable and that I hope they will use this to their advantage. It often does not take long for tables and chairs to be rearranged and new meeting areas to arise. Students congregate in the window sill or on pillows, or they pull chairs together to work together. They make the furniture and the room work for whatever type of learning they are engaged with. They will gather whatever they need and move their learning to their spot, quickly making the space work for them better than what it did before. The manipulation of space and how it affects their learning is also an ongoing conversation; how students face each other, how their body language comes across, and how they place their project items are all conversations waiting to happen. As we help our students grow as human beings, it is important that we offer students up a space where they can work well together, not based on what I think they need, but on what they know they need.

Do Students Have Room for Quiet?

Many teachers plan for flow and natural collaboration, but not as many plan for quiet. During our independent reading time every year, inevitably there is a child who moves far away from others and then tries to hide his or her whereabouts. I have had children build forts out of pillows to crawl into, hang jackets over desks, hide behind a propped open door, or even request to go into a separate team area. At first, I assumed it was so they could get out of reading; after all, if we are constantly on the prowl for the child who is not reading, then finding a place to hide is a great way to not get found out. Yet, after observation and conversation, I realized that these students were not trying to hide, they were trying to become immersed, and having spaces where they could seclude themselves naturally helped them to do that. I am not sure why I had not realized this sooner; I am a hermit reader myself, preferring absolute silence and stillness when I fall into the pages of a book. So as you plan your space, is it possible for students to remove themselves from others? Are there nooks and crannies that can be used as shields? With between one third and one half of the American population defining themselves as introverts, are we creating work spaces that function for them as well as our more extroverted students? (Cain 2012). Even in a square space with just tables and chairs, is there a way for us to create a physical distance between those who prefer learning to be more social and those who prefer it more quiet? I have even set out headphones in previous years for those who would like to use them unplugged as a way to create a sound barrier. What matters is that we discuss the types of noise we would like our learning community to be ensconced in and that we create a way for all people to function best if possible.

One winter, after receiving a small grant, I asked the students what we should spend the money on. I was expecting them to tell me more books—after all, we had a long shared wish list of books we could not wait to read. Rather quickly the consensus was clear; we need better seating and not just these plastic chairs. Mission accepted and thus armed with the school credit card, I went to my local superstore to see what I could find. Cheap yoga balls, exercise straps, pillows, and some plastic deck chairs all made it back into our learning community as I eagerly waited for the reaction of the students, hoping that these things were enough. The response was immediate; the gratitude over these few changes was vast. But best of all, I noticed that for many students, it now took them less time to concentrate on the learning, even if there was an awful lot of bouncing at hand those first few minutes. However, knowing that not all of my students want to bounce on a ball, I also kept regular chairs. As with any change, it is important that the change we make benefits as many as we can without excluding those whom it would deter from learning. When students have an opportunity to discover how they learn best, their learning is affected. When the environment they are in is conducive to them performing better because they feel more comfortable, the learning deepens, as do the relationships. And at the end of the day, relationships and how comfortable children feel in our learning environments is what will lead them to better reading experiences.

Questions to ponder as you consider learning community environment:

◆ How does your physical space influence your mood as an educator?
◆ How does your physical space influence the mood of your students?
◆ How does your physical environment support the learning?
◆ How does your physical environment hinder the learning?
◆ How can you make changes that will benefit everyone who uses the room?
◆ How do students manipulate the environment?
◆ What, if any, furniture can be removed?
◆ How can a love of reading be reflected in the classroom environment?

3

The Classroom Library
as the Cornerstone of the Passionate
Reading Community

Teachers should have classroom libraries because kids need to be able to see
good books right in front of them, otherwise they will never look at them.
—Claudia, seventh grader

To anyone who enters our room, it is clear that books are important. As I've
mentioned, books are overtaking our space more and more. Why is the classroom library so significant, not only to our young readers but also to our
older ones? For starters, it would be harder, though not impossible, to create a
passionate reading learning community without the presence of one. In fact,
in a study done by Linda Gambrell called *Creating Learning Community Cultures That Foster Reading Motivation*, it was concluded that the findings "suggest that book access is a significant factor in literacy development and that
greater attention should be devoted to assuring that high-quality classroom
libraries are a priority in schools." In fact, NCTE released a position statement
in May, 2017 declaring that "Classroom libraries—physical or virtual—play a
key role in providing access to books and promoting literacy; they have the
potential to increase student motivation, engagement, and achievement and
help students become critical thinkers, analytical readers, and informed citi-
zens." Over the years, as I have advocated more loudly for classroom libraries
at all grade levels, I have been asked why not just rely on the school library?
Why spend the extra resources on books for a few when that same money
can be diverted and be spent on books for the many? My rationale is simple

and twofold. One, we need books right in front of our students. The moment they either abandon or finish a book outright, they need to be inspired to pick up their next read. That can only happen when books are in their presence at all times. Two, it should never be an either/or situation, but always a both. As educators, we must advocate and validate the need for not only a well-stocked school library staffed with a full-time librarian, but also a well-stocked classroom library. Our students deserve to have access to books in multiple places, to have access to more than one reading role model, and to have access to more books than they could ever imagine reading. The research agrees, according to Library Research Services, "Studies conducted over the past two decades . . . show that students in schools with endorsed librarians score better on standardized achievement tests in reading, compared with students in schools without endorsed librarians."[1]

Now take that knowledge of a librarian and combine it with a knowledgeable teacher who also provides access to books and think of the long-term gains that can follow.

Depending on where you look, the research on quantity of books needed differ; however, one thing is clear—we should all have books present in our classrooms. The American Library Association recommends about 300 stand-alone titles, supplemented by a fully functioning school library (Huck, Hepler, and Hickman 1993; Neuman 1999). The International Literacy Association recommends a starting point of at least seven books per child, with the purchase of two more books every year per child. That may seem impossible for us as secondary teachers, as that might mean upwards of 800 books to start out with, depending on how many students one teaches. Yet I find it to be a great goal to shoot for in the long run, and then hopefully, at some point, surpass it. Fountas and Pinnell recommend 300–500 titles, depending on the grade level taught (1996). What this means for us, wherever we are on our journey of book procurement, is that we need classroom libraries. And not just books, but good books, books that students want to read so that all of our students can feel like Sam did when he wrote, "I'm reading more this year because of all the book choices that are right at my fingertips."

Yet building a strong classroom library with enough books to reach all of our readers is not an easy task, because how do we, in our cash-strapped schools, advocate for more books? How do we reach these recommended levels of libraries when we might be the ones purchasing all of the books? While there is no easy answer, my book spending is greater than any of my other monthly purchases. I think we should also remember that our libraries do not need to be large to be effective, at least not at first. In fact, I would rather have students exposed to a small library that is filled with great-quality books than one that is filled with books but offer little in the shape of stellar reading experiences. So we can spend our own money wisely, seeking out only the best-of-the-best books by paying attention to what is shared through online sources, asking our students what they see the need for, and becoming more connected with other readers ourselves. We can take a pledge to purchase better books for our own libraries and know that with our purchases, we are investing in the future generation. As administrators, we can look at where our funding is spent. Is money set aside for adequate classroom libraries, or is the money gone after curricular programs or technology has been purchased? It makes little sense to me to spend thousands of dollars on a program that teaches reading comprehension if little to no money is spent on the books handed to students to help them love reading. Through selective book purchasing, and with a focus of quality above quantity, we can therefore try to ensure that when children go to book shop, they can find a few great books in the time they browse, not spend their whole time finding "maybes." To do that, though, we need to know our library and the needs of our readers. That is why the components of a passionate reading environment is not one that solely rests on the teacher as a reading role model, or the student as a passionate reader, or the learning community as a well-functioning component, but on all three working together to create the desired experience. If I had only realized that when I first started out, creating my own classroom library.

Then—A Fully Stocked Library That Hardly Anyone Used

Having a variety of books allows students to choose which book fits their personality best.

—Emma, seventh grader

Several years ago, I had a classroom library that was filled to the brim with books. Every shelf crammed. Every space occupied, yet every independent reading time it never failed; a student would ask if he or she could please go to the library to find a book. I did not think twice about it. Of course, they could go to the library, where else would they get books? Yet, one day it finally did strike me as odd; why in the world were the students not going to our library first to see all the books there? There were great books on the shelves; there had to be, right? I mean, I am sure there was, they just had to find them first. And that was exactly it—our library was full. Full of leftover books I had picked up when other teachers weeded. Full of books picked up from our local goodwill store and garage sales. A few random selections from Scholastic bonus points that did not really fit my students. Full of books inherited when the teacher before me had left the room. Full of books with torn covers, broken spines, and even a few missing pages, I am sure. The library was full and not many were using it.

The library itself was also not well organized. I had books in bins, but the genre labels on them were very broad or too narrow. I did not do much in marketing of the library either; book talks were few and far between and books were rarely on display. When I look back at pictures of my old classrooms, I notice how few books are present in the images. Now whenever a picture is snapped in our classroom, it is hard to not have a book in it. Yet I did have a carpet, I did have accessible bookshelves. I did have a return system and somewhat of an organizational system, so the disarray of the library was not inherently obvious to a casual onlooker, and I think that is why it took me so long to discover how little it was used. It looked used, but mostly because those children who did not know what to read, would reach for whatever book they needed at the moment to at least pretend they were reading. It looked used because a few committed readers would take the time to book shop deeply in our Friday morning slot, and so those kids would return books and replace them. Yet for the most part, my students would rather not read or wait to find a book from somewhere else.

Upon realizing how little used our classroom library was, I did the unthinkable; I threw out books. I got rid of all of those books that no child had read for years. The ones with the covers falling off, the ones that even I would not read. I got rid of the old, the broken, and even sometimes the new. The too mature. The unwanted and the forgotten. And then I stood back and looked at my distinctly smaller library, wondering what to do next. Because now I had a half-empty library, and my problem was not solved. There still were not many great books to discover and read. As stated previously, research says different things on how many books we need in our learning community libraries. Some say twenty books per child. Others say between 300 and 600 total. But the number does not matter if the books are not good. So instead of focusing on quantity, which was a lost cause anyway since I had not won the lottery, I focused on quality. I focused on getting high-interest books in the hands of my students. I focused on purchasing a few great books when I could so that students would encounter great reading experiences whenever they browsed our library. I started small but purposeful and book talked the books that were added so that students knew that now these books were worth their time. Slowly but surely our library grew, and it continues to do so to this day. With a now fully stocked library, I am therefore often asked, how do you know which books to purchase?

I Ask the Students

Paying attention was not enough, so I started asking them which books they liked to read and have continued to do so throughout my teaching years. Such a simple question, yet one that has had the biggest results. They started to speak books with me so that I could see what books meant to them. This continues to be one of the biggest ways I figure out what to read; by asking questions, by paying attention, and by always seeking out recommendations. To this day, students will email me recommendations, tell them to me as I pass them in the hallway, or leave me post-it reminders on my desk. In fact, one of the final speeches of our year is now "The Best Book of the Year," in which the students share their love of a book while I furiously scribble down all of the titles mentioned, adding them to my ever-expanding wish list.

I Hand Them Scholastic Catalogs

For all of those books that we have not read yet, I need to know what looks good to them. So I ask them to circle the ones that catch their attention and they hand the catalogs back to me. If more than one child circled a book, I know it would probably be a good buy. I also take better advantage of all of the bonus point deals from Scholastic and I tell parents what my plans are. More parents purchase books so we can earn more points, and when we fall short, I fund the difference, because let's face it, that's what we do as teachers.

I Ask Them to Weed

While I have done purges of books without my students, I do love involving them in the process. Especially as we now have a larger library, and I have many more students and their reading preferences to keep track of. Often I will pull the books I am looking to give away or get rid of altogether, but then ask students to go through the piles for me. They then have the option to save a book if they would like. This is also a way for us to inspire more book conversations in our learning community. Sometimes the very books that look outdated are the most beloved; all it takes is for the right child to pick it up and book talk it to the class for others to want to read it. It was, and is, amazing to see students discover a long-forgotten book and rush to share with friends, insisting that they read it.

I Read Their Books

While I had never stopped being a reader when I began teaching, I was not a reader of children's books. I had not browsed the children's or teen section of our local bookstore, and I had not familiarized myself with what people under the age of 18 were reading. This meant I had nothing to recommend to my students. So I started by asking them what I should read and then took them up on their recommendations, eagerly sharing my own progress with the child who gave me the initial recommendation. This is a tactic I use to this day; I ask for ideas of what to read next, and the students gladly oblige. When I finish a book, I book talk it and leave it out for the kids to read. Sometimes

I hand it to a specific student that I thought of while I read it. There is no possible way for me as a teacher who loves reading to help students develop a better relationship with reading if I do not read the books that are meant to help them fall in love with reading. I would miss out on most of the pieces that we build our relationship on if I did not take the time to read "their" books. Besides buying books for our learning community, actually reading them myself is one of the biggest investments, and commitments, I have ever made. As Stephen Krashen wrote, "Children read more when they see other people reading" (2009), and I would say the same goes for when they have a teacher in their midst who can speak books with them.

I Use the Public Library

Those librarians know a thing or two about amazing children's books, so I started to pay attention. What do they have on display? What do they recommend? I also borrow books and read them before I decide what to buy. I still do this a lot with the picture books I buy. I also use our local bookstores more. What do they have on display? What is popular for them? Use the knowledgeable people that surround you. A great service to use is netgalley.com, which allows you to request free e-book versions of up-and-coming books. This is a great way to familiarize yourself with what is out there and also take a book on a test ride before you purchase it.

I Am Friends With My Fellow Book Lovers

I have had the honor of working with some incredible librarians that love books as much as I do. And yet, I hardly ever spoke about books with them. What a wasted opportunity. So find out who the book lovers are in your school and befriend them if you have not already. Talk books whenever you can. I now have a tribe of book-loving colleagues who have no problem talking books whenever we can. We swap books, we send messages about books, and we help each other find great books for certain students. This is what being in a passionate reading community is all about.

I Invest Time in the Nerdy Book Club

Being connected online to fellow bibliophiles is an incredible gift we can give ourselves. Finding our tribe, who will obsess over books, who will recommend, who will share, who will even ship books to one another is something I hope every teacher gets to experience. In finding the Nerdy Book Club, I found my tribe of people who loved books, who had books to recommend, who knew just what books to invest in. To this day, the Nerdy Book Club is one of the only blogs that is delivered straight to my inbox so I don't miss a single post (https://nerdybookclub.wordpress.com/).

I Pay Better Attention and I Speak Less

I spend a lot of time really noticing what my students are reading, what they are abandoning, and what they seem to read but then not read as their eyes drift around the room. We also speak a lot about the books we love and why. While there are many reasons why I want to hear students speak books, one of them is that through their conversations I can look for books similar to the ones they are professing their love for, adding them to our library as we go. Stepping back and out of the conversation is vital as we try to create a community of book lovers; we should be a voice, yes, but not the main voice as the year unfolds. Creating a community of book lovers is something that takes time, takes commitment, and will not just happen on its own. The students have so much to share if only we ask them.

I Frequent the Best-Kept Secret

I still remember the moment I was told about Books4School.com, a warehouse here in Madison, Wisconsin, that sells brand new overstock books for less than $2. Yup. And not random titles either, but books my students want to read, by authors like Cassandra Clare, John Green, Rick Riordan, and so many others. While their only physical location is here, they also sell online and just as cheaply. Trust me, the deals are worth it, and their stock changes all the time.

I Take My Responsibility for Diverse Representation and Experiences Seriously

Dr. Rudine Sims Bishop's monumental work about books serving as windows and mirrors is something that has transformed and guided my book purchases (Bishop, 1990). Teaching a White majority student population has made me acutely aware of how many experiences my students may never have been subjected to, for better or for worse. As their English teacher, it is therefore vital that I immerse them in literature that will not only allow them to see themselves represented (the mirror), but also familiarize themselves with other cultures, lifestyles, or life experiences (window). In the last few years, I have seen the addition of the door to the analogy, meaning that our literature choices must afford children a chance to step into a new experience, and I wholeheartedly agree. We carry a social responsibility to make sure that not only are all of our students and their life experiences represented in our libraries, but so are those whose lives do not mirror ours in the slightest.

Many years ago I realized that while our library was full, it was not great. It was not something the students could use. It was not something they wanted to use. So I embarked on a journey to get better books in the hands of my students. I found a better way to spend the precious money we have to get books for our libraries. And it worked. Slowly, our library has grown to now encompass more than 2,000 books. Books that the students want to read. Books that are worn out from use and not from age. Getting rid of books is one of the best decisions I made for our library, even though it was a painful one and still is when I continue to weed titles. Yet, in the end, I have discovered that it is not always about the number of books waiting for the students, but the quality of the experience that is waiting for them.

Looking Beyond Our Own Interests

If my classroom library were for me, there would be no dog books. Well, almost no dog books, because *Rain Reign* deserves to be there. There would be no sports books, except for maybe *Stupid Fast*. There would be no books with mermaids, unicorns, or any kind of princess, except for the feisty ones. If my classroom library were for me, I would have only books that I know would fit all of my readers, that no one would ever object to or question. I would take the easy way; after all, who needs more worries in their life?

There would be shelves and shelves of dystopian science fiction mixed with a little bit of love. There would be historical fiction but mostly the more recent stuff. Realistic fiction would be a major section, but fantasy would be reserved for the stuff that makes sense, after all, who needs books about dragons?

But it is not

Our classroom library is filled with dog books. With books about kings and queens, footballs, and dragons. It is filled with books about men who went to war and never came back, and about women who conquered the world. It is filled with science, with history, and even with joke books, because who doesn't need a good laugh now and then?

Our classroom library is not just for me. It serves more than 130 students, and some may have similar tastes as me, but most of them don't. So when I choose whether a book deserves a spot in our library, I cannot just think of myself. I cannot be afraid to place books in it that scare me. I cannot be afraid of what others may think if I know that a book is needed. I cannot use myself as a measuring stick. If I did, our library would not be for the students.

So when we purchase books and when we decide what to display, what to book talk, and what to remove, keep this in mind—our classroom libraries are meant to be homes to all readers. Not just the ones that are like ourselves. Not just the ones who have seemingly quiet lives filled with normal things like family dinner and soccer. Not just the ones who love to read. Not just the ones who tell us which books to buy and raise their hand when we ask who wants to read it next.

Our classroom libraries are for all kids that enter our learning community. Especially for the ones who are lost, who have not found that book or that story that made them believe that they are readers, that their life matters. We must have books that allow all children to feel that way. To feel like there is not something wrong with them. It is no longer a matter of just having diverse books, it is about having the right books for all those kids who come to us and wonder whether they are normal, whether they are okay, and then displaying those books. The books speak for us, so make sure they speak loudly. Make sure that in your classroom children can find that book that will make the biggest difference. Make sure you do not stand in the way. Make sure fear of what others may think does not stop you from helping a child come one step closer to liking reading.

Now—A Library Come Alive

Teachers should definitely make their classroom libraries accessible and easy to use. They should have a diversity of books, chapter, picture books, comic books and easy reads. They should organize their books by genre and even put together a classroom favorite list.

—Amber, seventh grader

After six and a half years as an elementary teacher, accepting a seventh grade English job was terrifying. Teaching children only two years older should not have been that scary, yet it was, because so much changes in those few years between the ages of 10 and 12. So as I started to pack up my fifth grade classroom, deciding what to bring or what to leave behind, it took me only about three seconds to decide that I was going to move my entire classroom library into my new school and classroom. Coming from fifth grade, I wasn't quite sure what the use of a classroom library would be on my new adventure; after all, we would only have 45 minutes together, but I could not leave my books behind. I could not leave them in boxes. Even if we did not need the books as a class, I needed them. My books were home to me, and when you change schools, when you change districts, when you change grade levels, you need all of the pieces of home you can find. Yet, I did not recall seeing large or even many classroom libraries in the middle and high schools I had visited, so perhaps there were not really needed at this age group? Either way, my husband, Brandon, carried every single box of books into my new classroom. There were more than sixty of them, and they took up an entire wall as I waited for my bookshelves to arrive. A few weeks later, as I opened each box and shelved the books in their new home, I could not help but wonder if any child would ever read them. If dust would soon become their norm rather than being in the hands of children. Was there any point in my meticulous placement of these books or would they sit in their bins mocking me as the students walked right past them?

On the first day as a seventh grade teacher, I remained unsure as to how the students would react to the books. After all, in younger grades, most kids expect a classroom library. Most kids are used to the access. Many will naturally go to check out the classroom library as a part of their first day of school, but perhaps middle schoolers had outgrown that curiosity. I needn't have worried, because shortly into our very first day together, these terrifyingly huge 12-year-olds released their welcome comments. "Are these all of your books?" "Have you read them all?" "How many books do you have?" "Can we read them?" Slowly, they became more poignant. "How do I check this one out?" "Can I read this one?" "Did you read this book? I have wanted to read it." It turns out my worry was unfounded. It turns out that some middle schoolers in all of their bravado love classroom libraries as much as younger kids. That some middle schoolers get as much use out of a classroom library as they did in the younger years if we let them. That they all need books now just as much as they needed them then, even if they never in a million years will admit it to you. In the past few years as a seventh grade teacher, therefore, our classroom library has only grown. Teaching more than 130 students quickly made me realize just how many books I need to keep all readers invested and engaged with their reading. In fact, I started with the research on classroom library sizes and knew that while these were great starting points, they were exactly that, a start. When you teach that many students with reading abilities ranging from second to twelfth grade and interests spanning all topics, you need way more than you think, because middle schoolers are developing and fine-tuning their reading preferences. So the message that my classroom library sends is that there is always another book waiting, there is always another chance at falling in love or remaining in love with reading.

My devotion to our classroom library is not because we do not have a school library, we have a beautiful one; one that is filled with incredible books and staffed with incredible people. But when the students are with me, during our 45 minutes of instruction every day, they also need books right at their fingertips. As Donalyn Miller and Teri Lesesne have said, "Even a school library right across the hall from you is too far away for many students" (NCTE conference presentation, 2015). And it is true, even a beautiful, well-stocked school library is too far away when a child needs a book right then. Because our students need to be enticed by another book the moment they finish or abandon their current one. They need books as a way to create community as they share their love (or dislike) of them with others. They need books to hand to their friends, to their teachers. They need books that will inspire them to read more. To discover who they are as readers and who they want to become. They need to be able to go into our library and come out with something that speaks to them. Not just because the teacher tells them they have to read or the assignment requires them to. They need books that are more than okay, that urge them to read just one more page, that continue to tell them that they may not be readers just yet, but there is still hope for them. Every year as I ask students what they wish all teachers of reading would do, the majority of students answer that they wish they would all have a classroom library like ours. I agree, ours is one of luxury, of large amounts of my own money spent, that is impressive in its size, and continues to grow even as I write this. I know how lucky I am that I am in a situation where I can get more books in the hands of my students. Where I can create a book flood for them, to quote Kelly Gallagher (*Readicide*, 52). And yet, it is not the size, I think, that draws my students back to our library, it is the quality of the books. So while our students pine for large classroom libraries, they are also perfectly happy settling for smaller ones that can grow. For smaller ones that have great books in them, for smaller ones carefully curated by a teacher who loves reading.

Component of Change: Rethinking the Classroom Library

Most people don't have a lot of books at home and you only go to the [school] library once every two weeks. [When we have a classroom library] kids have access to books they want to read and do not have to wait to get a book.

—Kennedy, seventh grader

As we increase the demand on students to read for knowledge and tasks rather than pleasure, we see their love of reading decline. Students have less time and less choice as they go through their years of schooling, and as we expect more of them academically, we remove more choice and control over much of their academic involvement, including the books they read. This is leading us into an aliteracy crisis, where adults are not reading not because they can't read, but because they do not want to. According to a report published by the National Endowments for the Arts, "the steepest decline in reading is in the youngest age groups; 18–24" (National Endowments for the Arts Reading at Risk, www.arts.gov/sites/default/files/RaRExec.pdf). These are the adults who have just left our educational system and are now free to choose to not read, rather than to read whatever they want. But we can fight against this. The need for a proper classroom library in our middle and high school learning communities is therefore not a frivolous thrill; it is a vital necessity to create passionate reading environments. Having a classroom library should not be an investment we only make for our younger students, but should be one we make for all students, no matter their age. We have seen a disturbing

Image 3.1 Picture books for all

downward trend in reading scores for adolescents, and while test scores are not the be all and end all, I think they do shed a light on a larger problem in this case—children who are not enjoying reading as much as they did in the earlier grades and therefore do not care about what a test asks them (NAEP 2015). Having a fully stocked classroom library that will entice students to read at all times is therefore of utmost importance. It is not too late to start right now. We start by buying one book, then another, and we build our collection day by day. We book talk and we hand books to students. We create displays that entice and time to read, but first we have to have the books and access to them for all the kids we teach.

Our collection now probably holds more than 2,000 chapter books and more than 500 picture books, and yet I know that I still do not have enough. After all, there are still students that search our shelves and come up empty-handed, but at least they have books to browse, at least they have books to try. I continue to add whenever I can, knowing that one day I will run out of wall space and bookshelf space. But when that day comes, it will be a day of celebration, because perhaps we now have a book for every interest, for every reader, for every child we teach. So how do you begin and where do you begin? Or, how do you continue on the book procurement journey you have already been on? For a functioning classroom library, I believe there are a few pillars that need to be in place: inspiring books, ease of access and check out, and a social component. So what have been the successful components of our classroom library? As one student said on our end-of-year survey, "I wish that every teacher had a big library so I don't run out of books on my to-be-read list."

Be a Spokesperson for Your Classroom Library

Besides independent reading time, we do not hold many things sacred in our classroom. In fact, most things can be adapted or squished in order to book talk a great book or show a new book trailer. That is simply the reality of teaching English language arts within the 45-minute framework; you never have enough time, so you make every minute count. Infusing my passion for books into our learning community may seem strange to my new students, but by the middle of the year the students know if I am not feeling well, based on a reading slump on the lack of book talks. We talk books, it is what we do, and we also share books, write about books, and browse books whenever we can. And while it may not always be on the agenda as a focal point, not a day passes without a student and me discussing their reading choice or lack of one. It is not that we need to create learning communities where students are dependent on the teacher as their reading guide, but we need to create ones where we can start with those children who do not identify as readers or

Image 3.2 Picture books are always on display to entice for quick reading

who do not read for fun and empower them to move further on their reading journey. We must become the bridge builder, as those children set out on a quest toward a more meaningful reading experience. We must be the ones that show that we cannot live without the presence of books. Not in a competitive sense, while we showcase our vast number of books read, but instead in a way of saying that reading is a necessary part of being a fully functioning human being. We know that being a reader gives you an advantage in many areas in life, such as having more empathy, being less stressed, making you feel more connected, and keeping your brain younger longer (Gelman n.d.). So we must be the ones who spotlight, who recommend, who take care of our books (with help from the students, of course), and also who continue to pursue the best connections and opportunities for students as they try to find books that they will love. We must be relentless. We must be passionate. We must be unapologetic. And we must be kind.

So when I realized that our library was more filled with dust than with books being read, I knew that it was not just a matter of getting better books, but also of changing my role. I no longer assumed that students would discover the great books we had or take the time to browse, but instead became an exuberant spokesperson for our library. I made it a point to talk about the library. I made it a point to pull bins out and show students stacks of books they might love. I made a big deal of placing new books into the library, showing book trailers, sharing my review, asking for guest reviewers, asking for students to love the classroom library as well and use it all of the time. I searched for the students who would naturally become spokespeople for our classroom library and gave them a platform to be heard; after all, not every child we teach despises reading. The library is now something we cherish and uphold. Students from other rooms and grades borrow books from it as well; they know they can probably find something. Gone is the dust, gone are the broken bins and broken spines. In its place are, books and lots of love—for reading, for sharing, and for exploring.

Questions to ponder as you develop your own classroom library vision:

- ◆ How often is the classroom library discussed and highlighted?
- ◆ When was the last time you weeded out books?
- ◆ How can your classroom library become a vibrant component of your learning community?
- ◆ How can you give often overlooked books more attention?
- ◆ How can you make speaking about the classroom library part of your everyday or weekly routine?
- ◆ How can you help students understand the inherent value it possesses?
- ◆ How can you get students who do not gravitate toward books to use the classroom library?

Create Displays That Entice

The day of winter break one year, I cleared all of our books from their display areas and neatly put them away. As my last class of the day entered the room, they stood in mild surprise. "What happened?! What is wrong with you?!" I soon discovered the cause of their urgent dissatisfaction; the removal of their recommended books. As seventh graders do so well at times, they told me loudly how they hated it and could I please put up some books? Taking care in displaying books well is something that I love. Much as our bookstores and librarians know how to create visually pleasing displays, I think we must take the time to do so as well in our classrooms. I am not a crafty person, so my displays tend to revolve around themes. I do not make bulletin boards to go with them because I have no space. But I do pull entire collections out and place them around the room. I take care in displaying books that highlight many different people, backgrounds, and cultures, because in our displays we are once again offering students a chance to read stories that do not always reflect their own experience. Exposing students to diversity through their text experiences and also critically evaluating the experience they have with the text are of great importance to me. Our picture book displays rotate through-out the years in order to entice more kids to read the books. I go through my clear plastic bins once in a while and pull new books to the front for students to see. I point out when displays are changed, because it is never guaranteed that the students will notice it. Books are continually put on display as they come in and new books are often kept hidden until we book shop (more on that in the coming chapters). The students see the pile next to the wall grow and start to ask when they can see them. So if we have a clear surface that is not needed for a workspace, then I think placing a book on it, eager to be read, is a wonderful way of using it.

Questions to ponder as you reflect on your book displays:

- What was the last book display you created?
- Who creates the book displays?
- Do students notice when new displays are created?
- Who or what is represented in your displays?
- When are book displays used as a part of your teaching?
- How can you find more room to display more books?
- How can students take ownership over the book displays?

Organize Well

Keeping a library well organized is nearly as important as having great books. If students cannot find the books they are searching for, or if the library does not invite them to browse, then we may as well not invest in all of the books to begin with. Therefore, think strategically. When you go to a bookstore or a beautiful public library, what do you notice? How do the employees entice you to pick up all of those books? How do you browse yourself? These are all things that should be considered as you present and sort your library. Now, a word of reality. I have metal shelves that line our walls; those are my only options. I do not worry anymore about the look of the shelves, but rather the book displays themselves, and I make sure that books are at the front of our room, rather than hidden in the back. All of our shelves are therefore toward the natural front of the room and well lit. This is important, because we want students to inherently understand what the impact of books will have on our learning experience. It therefore makes sense to put them in an area that receives natural attention, or to draw attention to them in some other way, such as through the use of lighting, carpet, or alternative seating.

For a long time, I had a wire rack on which I placed all of my favorite books for students to browse. Yet, it was not being used very much, even though it was in a prime location. After inspiration by Nancie Atwell in her milestone book *The Reading Zone*, I hung a sign above it declaring it a rack for the students to share their favorite books and then took all of my books off. I told the students its new purpose and have since watched it fill up with their favorite reads. This spinning rack has now become the first stop whenever they need a new book.

However, organization is not just a matter of where you place your bookshelves; it is also a matter of what system you use for students to find a certain genre or format of book. This has been a work in progress for me throughout the years. I started with an alphabetically organized library and quickly gave that up, and then moved to plastic bins the size of shoe bins, which is still what I use the most. While they cost money and give you less shelf space, it has proven to be the easiest way for us to categorize books. Every bin is labeled with an address label, and I hand-write the label. I used to print them out, but found it to be more work than necessary. All labels are written as best as I can. The label will have the genre, format, or author, as well as the abbreviation used for that genre or author. (To see all of the genres we have in our classroom library, see appendix). Bins are grouped by genre, format, or popular authors. Students suggest bins as well, as they see a certain collection grow. Two such examples are our newly formed personal struggles bins and military history bins, after students pointed out that we had a collection now and they needed their own home. I try to buy the bins on sale and always keep some on hand in case a new bin needs to be created. I also give up bins if the books are no longer being read. This is the case for most of our author bins. After discussion with my students, they told me they typically would not browse an author bin and asked me to place the books into the regular bins instead. We kept a few very famous author bins (J. K. Rowling, Rick Riordan, and such) but immersed other author bins into the rest of the library. The effect was immediate—books that had gathered dust in their author bins were now being checked out. So discuss this with your students; are author bins being used, if no, why not? In fact, paying attention to which bins are being visited most will clue you into popular reads in your classroom. I have also found that which shelves you place the bins on makes a difference, so pay attention to where students go to look for books and use it to your advantage. I know that I can place our graphic novel bins anywhere in the room and the students will find them, so I often put other less-visited bins by them to up their readership. It works every time.

Another easy idea for better book organization has been the purchase of a book stamp to make sure books are returned when finished. Now, whenever a new book enters our learning community, it is stamped on the inside cover with a stamp that reads "This book belongs to Mrs. Ripp, please return when finished," and right below there I write the genre abbreviation. I will often write several genre abbreviations such as RF/PS/SPO, which stands for realistic fiction/personal struggle/sports. That way, when books are shelved they can go in any of those categories. Because the system is the same for every book—students know to look on the inside right cover to see where a book belongs. Having my name in the book has also saved many books from being lost over the years, and the stamp that I purchased for less than 10 dollars continues to be one of the best investments I have ever made.

Questions to ponder as you reflect on your organization:

◆ How are your books organized currently?
◆ Does the system work for all?
◆ Can students use the library independently and find the book they are looking for?

Image 3.3 Picture books are organized by the first letter of the authors last name

- How much time is spent reorganizing?
- How much time is spent searching for that one book?
- Do you have room for more books or are you limited in space?

Include Genres and Then Subgenres

Another one of the more recent changes spurred on by my students is the introduction of subgenres; collections of books that not only share a common genre, such as nonfiction, but also a more narrow category such as "Life Stories" (a subgenre we created for all of those biographies that are written about ordinary people whom extraordinary things happened to). This has resulted in students having an easier time finding a book they would like to read because many of my students, at least by the end of the year, have found certain niches that they like to explore. The idea of subgenres also came from the wisdom of both educator and author Penny Kittle and my colleague Reidun Bures, who have used it with success in their learning communities. So while we still have a few bins labeled "Realistic Fiction," we also now have bins labeled "Death and Dying," which is one of the most popular subgenres in our learning community, "High School Experiences," "Personal Struggles," and so on. As themes emerge among common texts, we create a new subgenre for them to call home. Books may therefore also have more than one

Image 3.4 Our favorite books

Images 3.5 and 3.6 Subgenre bins

genre abbreviation inside their covers, so students will know that they can go in different bins.

Another new addition to our library is the blending of informational text and fiction on the same shelves. While the genre abbreviations are different, I wanted to allow students more fluidity when they go from fiction to nonfiction, so putting the same categories next to one another makes sense. Sports biographies therefore now stand with sports fiction books. Historical fiction books now stand next to actual history books. By mixing the two formats, in the same labeled bins even, I hope to increase the cross-format reading that creates more well-rounded reading experiences. It makes sense for us as adults to seek out both fiction and nonfiction texts on a topic we are interested in, so why not give students the same easy invitation into that experience?

Questions to ponder as you reflect on genrefication:

- What collections do you have of books right now?
- How are books grouped?
- What are your major genres?
- What are subgenres you could create?
- What are genres that seem to not be checked out?
- Do some genres need a new name to stir up interest?
- What would students call the genres—hint: ask them!

Embracing an Easy Checkout System

While there are many wonderful apps and checkout systems out there, I decided a few years ago to stop with a checkout system. Especially when teaching many students, who sometimes come and grab books while I am teaching, not having a system has allowed me to not be interrupted as much. While I have thought of creating an easy checkout system using technology, I am not sure it will actually save more books than what I use right now. However, in the spirit of experimentation during the writing of this book, I did just that. I downloaded an app and started scanning all of my books. I even told my students that they now would have to use an iPad to check out the books. While my students were totally fine with the change, I soon discovered that when a student returned a book, I had to return it under their name rather than just scan the book title back in. This little step is one I do not have time for, nor do I have knowledge of who had the book. As quickly as we tried the checkout system, we scrapped it again. I would rather lose a few books than lose that much time in my day figuring out which students just returned a book without checking in with me first.

I used to have students shelve the returned books, but I always ended up having to remind them and then reteach them how to get them in the right bin, even though everything was marked. I now have a plastic tub with a "Return your books here" sign taped to it right by all of our bookshelves. Once a day I take the time myself to shelve all of the returned books, because it gives me a way to see what is popular, look for books other students are wanting, and check on the conditions of some of our most beloved books. It takes me less than five minutes, and all the books are in the right bin and I have just been given insight into what is being read, or abandoned, in our learning community.

Therefore, we continue with our tried-and-true system; when students ask me what our checkout system is, I tell them to find a book they want to read and then to bring it back when they are done. Yes, I lose books every year, but I also lost books when I had a checkout system. I always hope that whatever book is lost has found itself a new home and is being read by a child who loves it. There is an asterisk to our checkout system though. If children would like to borrow a hardcover book, they are asked to remove the dust jacket and place a post it with their first and last name on it and then leave the dust jacket behind. I collect the jackets and hang on to them until the book is returned. This has greatly reduced the number of lost hardcover books, which tend to be our most expensive books. Students appreciate that checkout is so easy, they can grab and go and do so gladly, even if a class is in session. I want students to have easy access to books at all times—this does that for me. One thing to mention, though, is that our picture books are generally not allowed to be checked out unless there are special circumstances, such as a younger sibling. Since picture books are so easily read in our learning community, they do not need to be read at home. Having an easy checkout system means that students can quickly book shop when needed, whether I am there or not. In the end, I would rather see all of our books being read than sitting pristinely on a shelf.

Questions to ponder as you reflect on your checkout system:

- Is your current checkout system in need of an overhaul?
- Does your current checkout system cause you unnecessary work or stress?
- Can you streamline your current checkout system to save you time?
- Can students independently check out books or are you always needed?
- Does your current checkout system work for all students?

Make Multiple Copies Available

While I do have multiple copies of books in some of the bins, to free up space I sometimes pull the extra copies and keep them in my book club closet; a closet with designated space for our sixty or so book club choices. I let students know, though, that I have multiple copies of certain books, because some students would like to read a book with a friend. These self-created and unimposed book partnerships are encouraged throughout the year, and I often will purchase an extra copy of a high-interest book or collaborate with the librarian. This also works well for students who would like to listen to an audio version of a book. They often listen along with a friend and then discuss the book as they go. Do you have books that you think would be great for a partner read? Find a way to designate them as such or keep a list and let students know about it. I have seen amazing conversations happen when two or more students choose to read the same book at the same time.

Questions to ponder as you reflect on the number of book copies you have:

◆ Which books would do well as a partner read?
◆ Which books might do well as a book club or literature circle choice?
◆ Which books beg to be read and discussed?
◆ Where can you store multiple copies of books?
◆ How will students know which books you have multiple copies of?

Embrace Picture Books

I don't remember when I fell out of love with picture books, but I do remember wondering why any teacher who did not teach young children would invest any money in them. After all, picture books are so expensive, and there is not much to them. With their brevity, they can really only be discovered once and then stand forgotten on a shelf, leaving little long-term reading enjoyment. No, I would rather invest my money in chapter books; that is where you get the most value. So picture books? Perhaps a few selected mentor texts stashed carefully away behind my teacher desk, waiting for their moment as a mentor text.

I don't remember when I fell back in love with picture books. Perhaps it was the first time students laughed out loud with me at *Chick and Pug*. Perhaps it was the first time students held their breath with me when I read *Pete & Pickles* out loud. Perhaps when I cried while I read *Ivan: The Remarkable True Story of the Shopping Mall Gorilla*. Perhaps it was when those kids that hated reading so much would ask if they could borrow some picture books so they could read to their little sister, and then tell me all about their night the very next day. Whatever happened, I now know that picture books belong in every learning community, for every reader, and that I showcase that love with the very first experience we have on our very first day together, something we will do many times throughout the year; the reading aloud of a picture book. This simple shared reading experience is one that carries weight as we gather for story time. Throughout summer, I carefully gather a few (or ten) picture books that I know my students might love, and as I invite the students to "come on over" (which becomes our signal for our read-aloud), I hold them up for them to choose. This is important. I want students to know, if even just subliminally, that the very first experience we have together is one chosen by them. As I read aloud the chosen story, I love the reactions that I see as the students let part of their nervousness over this new school year dissipate, and they slowly invest themselves in the story. Their posture changes, the mutterings stop, the smiles begin. This year, as I read aloud *Baa Smart Sheep* (Sommerset), I loved the reactions of the students—laughing, guffaws, and a lot of side conversations but all surrounding the book. As we finished, we sat there for a moment, happy to have shared this reading experience. Happy to have introduced these new children to a major component of our connected reading experience, our picture book collection and how we use it to create a passionate reading environment.

Questions to ponder as you reflect on the use of picture books in your learning community:

- How many picture books do you currently have available to students?
- How could you use the picture book format to teach your (mini) lessons?
- What would the addition of picture books signal to your students?
- How can students be inspired to read more due to the presence of picture books?

Learn to Let Go

This has been my biggest take away in having a classroom filled with books and readers. Sometimes you don't have to have a perfect system for it to feel perfectly fine. The students make our book-loving learning community their own, so they change the organization of books, the shelving of them, and even how we read them. I don't mind; I just have to let go sometimes and trust the students.

Questions to ponder as you reflect on your classroom library:

- How would students describe your classroom library?
- How is your classroom library used right now?

◆ How are books organized right now?
◆ What steps can you take to make your classroom library more enticing?
◆ What small changes can you make to help get more books in the hands of readers?
◆ Are picture books a naturally integrated component of your reading culture?
◆ How could picture books create a more powerful literacy experience?
◆ How would the introduction of subgenres help students better know themselves as readers?

Teaching With Picture Books; The How and the Why

Enter our classroom and you will immediately see the hundreds of picture books that surround us. These picture books, often in the hands of students, are one of the foundations of our learning community, a much-used teaching tool, and a thread that ties our community together. Yet the path to embracing picture books in this way was not one that I came upon easily; instead, it took the careful observation of children reading picture books, as well as inspiration from educators like Paul Hankins, Colby Sharp, and Jillian Heise, who showed me how picture books could transform our learning experience. So why is a large portion of our classroom space and library dedicated to picture books, a format of book not typically seen in learning communities for older students?

Picture Books Give Us a Common Language

I love how we can read a picture book and then refer back to it again and again as we weave our threads of community throughout the year. The students remember it, they read it again, and they reminisce about reading it. In a short amount of time, we create a foundation upon which the students can bond and a way for us to be a part of their world. Even within my 45 minutes of instruction time, I know I can at least read a picture book out loud, most days. And if you don't teach English, read one once in a while to create a shared experience; students need community in all classes, not just the literacy ones.

Picture Books Can Teach Us Complex Matters in a Simple Way

When my students became curious about the great Malcolm X, I read them *Malcolm Little*. When we spoke of the civil rights movement and the everyday segregation that happened, I read them *Ruth and the Green Book*. When they feel completely alone, I read them *The Invisible Boy*. When we have to talk about what our actions do to others, we read aloud *Each Kindness*, which with its less-than-perfect ending is a perfect mirror of what life is really like. These books don't offer all of the knowledge my students need, but they give us a chance to start the conversation. There are so many curriculum picture books out there waiting for us to embrace them for the knowledge they give us, not written for the young reader but for mature kids that can take the information and do something with it. Don't let your students miss out on this experience.

Picture Books Can Make Us Feel Successful When We Have Lost Our Way

I often teach students who don't think they will ever be strong readers. Who do not go home and read, who do not gravitate toward books, but instead spend our reading time flipping pages and waiting for the bell. I hand these kids stacks of picture books. I tell them to immerse themselves and come up when they are ready for more. While it may take a few attempts, inevitably the picture books win, and the child starts to read them rather than stare blankly into space. There is no judgment from other kids, nor jealousy. Our picture books are waiting for anyone to read them, no permission needed.

Picture Books Relieve Stress

If a child is having a bad day, I can hand them a stack of "Elephant and Piggie" books and know that at some point a small smile will form. I can hand them anything fantastical that is nothing like their real life and for a moment they have a reprieve. How often do our students get a chance to escape the stress of their lives and still work? Picture books offer me that opportunity.

Picture Books Can Make Us Believe That We Can Read Well

For the child who gave up a long time ago on reading. For the child who does not believe that school is for him or her. For the child who is angry, who is misplaced, who is lost; picture books can make the biggest difference. I once taught a student so angry he scared the rest of the class, but if I could get a stack of picture books in his hands before it was too late, send him to a quiet place, he de-escalated on most occasions. Picture books were not a threat, nor were they work. They were an escape and something that made him feel successful. If a child does not think they will ever read as well as the others, get them picture books, have them digest them slowly, see their progress, and see them start to believe that they too can be readers, that they too can belong. There is no shame in picture books, not when we embrace them fully as teachers. Not when we make them a part of our learning community. Remove the stigma so that students can find success within their pages, rather than feel there are no books for them out there.

How to Use Picture Books as a Teaching Tool

Which book I choose to share depends on the lesson. I treat it much like a short story in what I want students to get out of it, so it has to suit the very purpose we are trying to understand. I introduce the concept by sharing a personal story, such as when I had an important realization, and then I ask my students to come as close as they can to my chair in our corner. Once settled, whether on the floor, on balls, or on chairs, I read it aloud. We stop and talk throughout as needed but not on every page; it should not take more than 10 minutes at most to get through an average size picture book. If it is a brand new concept, I may just have students listen, while other times they might engage in a turn-and-talk. I have an easel right next to me, and at times we write our thoughts on that. Sometimes we make an anchor chart, it really just depends on the purpose of the lesson. Often a picture book is used as one type of media on a topic and we can then branch into excerpts from text, video, or audio that relates to the topic. Throughout my years, I have compiled lists of picture books that I use for teaching different concepts such as theme or plot (to access this list, please go to https://pernillesripp.com/our-favorite-books/).

Because I teach the same class five times in a row, I often switch out the picture books I use with the different classes. There are some that you can still love reading after four times, while others get to be a bit tedious, so I adjust as needed. This is why having a lot of great picture books to choose from is something I am committed to. I do not have multiple copies of any picture books, I don't see it as needed. Instead, I pick the picture book to read aloud and then find "companion books," other picture books that share the same concept; for example, easily identifiable themes. These are spread out on tables, waiting for the students to select them. This way, when I ask students to work with them they are truly testing out the skill and not just whether they can spot the same things that we just practiced together. Oftentimes, students can choose to work with a partner as they explore their self-selected books.

Sometimes students write after reading the picture books, other times they do not. Sometimes we use them as mentor texts where we mimic the way language is used or how a story is set up. I use them a lot as a way to do a quick check-in to see if students need reteaching or are on the right path. If students write about them, it tends to be just one paragraph or so. However, by including picture books as mentor texts, I am constantly exposing students to different types of writing and different types of content. Picture books therefore alleviate the need for a whole-class novel, as I can create a shared reading experience through their pages. That way we can all be invested in a short story, rather than run the risk of becoming disengaged with a longer one.

We do use some of the same picture books again and again as a way to practice close reading but also as a way to see different aspects of the same story. Once students have heard or read it to discover the story, we can focus on other things, such as language use or author's craft, as we rediscover it. This is a great way to get students to really look at how authors craft stories, both through written word but also in their illustrations. Depending on the book, we can mine it for many different writing lessons and expand our own repertoire as writers and as understanders of text.

Picture books tend to stay in the classroom because they get lost really easily; however, students may ask if they can borrow one to take home. Usually I say yes, as long as they bring it back the very next day. Due to the love of picture books, our middle school classroom library now has several hundred copies of some of the best picture books out there. Because our collection is vast, it had started to take me a good 10 minutes to find the particular book I needed at any given time. Since I know that the students like to grab and put them back quickly, I devised a simple system; every picture book gets a letter corresponding to the author's last name on its spine. That's it. Now they are filed by the subgroup of the letter, although not alphabetically within that letter, so finding that one really great book is super easy. Students can reshelve the picture books as needed, I can quickly find that picture book I need, and yet they are still within arm's reach, ready to be read. The small step of printing out a label for their spine takes me less than a minute but saves a lot of time in the end.

They are also displayed on top of every bookshelf and every ledge in our learning community; displays rotate as discussed previously. I also inherited gutters attached to one of my walls, and these make for perfect picture book displays. I am amazed at how often the students gravitate toward a picture book simply because I put it on display.

However, we do not just read picture books—they also serve as inspiration for our writing. For the past several years, my middle school students have written nonfiction picture books for younger audiences around the world. The goal of the project is rather simple; create a fifteen to twenty-five slide/page nonfiction picture book meant for a second or third grade audience on anything you wish to write about. Throughout this project, we have been able to successfully marry tech tools with writing, as well as use Skype, Padlet, Twitter, and other interactive tools.

Why this project? Because within it we have been able to work on:

- How to take organized notes in a way that works for them.
- How to write a paragraph and all of the myriads of lessons that are attached to that.
- Grammar! Spelling! Punctuation!
- How to find legal images.
- How to cite sources, including images, books, and websites.
- How to uncover reliable sources (yes, there is a place for Wikipedia in our research).
- How to search the internet better.
- How to conduct market research using Skype to ask second or third graders what they want to read and how they want to read it.
- How to rewrite information in our own words.
- How to do design and layout on a page to make it inviting.
- How to create good questions.
- Exploring our own interests.
- How to write assessment rubrics.
- How to work as a peer mentor group.
- How to monitor self-engagement.

Writing a picture book intended for an actual audience is a natural step for my students as they explore their own reading and writing identities. Inspired by the very books they read every day, they get to take part in the process that is required to be their own author, knowing that their final product will be read and enjoyed by others. The urgency that this brings to their writing and investment in the project cannot be matched by any other writing project we do, therefore by adding picture books into our classroom library we successfully reshape the entire literacy experience that all of my students have. (To see the full lesson plan for this project, please go to https://pernillesripp.com/2014/12/14/our-epic-nonfiction-project/.)

Note

1 www.lrs.org/documents/school/school_library_impact.pdf infographic

4

The Reality of the Passionate Reader Learning Community

Kids have voices too!
—Tessa, seventh grader

While I had incredible professors in college that tried their hardest to expose me to the reading research that I should build our reading experience on, as a newly minted teacher that experience was not enough. I had read the important texts from great minds like Fountas and Pinnell, Nancy Atwell, Ellin Keene, and others, but I did not know how I could create the environments that they discussed. I had the building blocks, but not the know-how of how to put it all together to fit the students I was to teach. So my first year as a teacher of fourth grade, I did what most new teachers do—I turned to my colleagues for help. They, after all, had more years of experience than I did and also had seemingly great ideas. I wanted to be seen as a team player, someone who did what was expected of her, even if my colleagues more than likely would have been just fine with me doing my own thing. I therefore followed their lesson plans in the most basic form by asking them what they were doing and then tried to emulate this. Most teachers know how this turns out; we become a shell of what those other teachers are because no matter how good of a lesson plan someone shares, when we have not infused our own experiences into it we can never emulate it well. Yet, as a first-year teacher, and even in subsequent years, I was too insecure in my own expertise as a teacher that I did not veer much off the path. I knew it could be better, my students' lack of passion for reading showed me that, but I did not know what better could be. So I went through the motions, hoping that someday I would figure it out. Yet, in those years, I was still teaching children whose future relationship with reading hinged on the year that they had with me. I took that responsibility seriously, as most teachers do, and yet it was not enough for me to realize that the book reports and day-by-day guided reading comprehension lessons were not hitting the heart of the matter—who they were as readers. I had to get beyond "this is not working," to figure out what would work for all of the readers I taught, whether they identified as such or not.

Those first few years of literacy, I followed the balanced literacy approach. This approach, defined as "a decision-making approach through which the teacher makes the thoughtful choices each day about the best way to help each child become a better reader or writer" (Spiegel 1998), was interpreted to mean using a whole-class novel, as well as book reports and projects spread throughout the year. I was not quite sure what else to do and was too overwhelmed to recognize the need to find out. Being a new teacher is an exhausting endeavor at any grade level, but at the elementary level where you are in charge of teaching multiple content areas, the realization of how little you know is a constant companion. At the upper levels, it is not that different except we often do not face the pressure of multiple content areas, but instead the lack of time. How do you teach everything when you only have 45 minutes? How do you successfully create meaningful literacy experiences when you do not have the luxury of long blocks of time to not only get to know your students and their needs better, but also to allow the students time to become better invested?

Knowing that you are, indeed, the master of none, especially as you begin your teaching career, means that you are constantly searching for the next day's better lesson, better way, better method, often failing to see the bigger picture of the day-to-day decisions you have made. I was no different. While I had the components of a literacy block, what I was doing was teaching reading at its most basic understanding; day-to-day comprehension lessons with support from worksheets and packets, because clearly a word search on a text will help a child love reading! Students were exposed to, and participated in, all of the things we know create great reading opportunities—read-aloud, guided reading, shared reading, and modeling— but on a surface level. As a brand new teacher, I simply did not know enough about creating successful reading experiences to thoughtfully select the components my students needed to become fully invested and connected readers. Even a few years in, with a few more years of teaching and reading research in my tool belt, I still did not know enough to really be a good teacher of reading, and doing these components as well as I could was not enough; it never would be. While balanced literacy speaks to many truths I hold dear in reading, the program, much like any program, is a scaffold meant to support us as we discover our own reading teacher identities, ones hopefully propelled by a passion for reading as we continue on our mission to help all children become readers. The program is a great place to start, but we must go beyond it to create deeply personal and meaningful experiences within our classrooms. One missing component in the balanced literacy model was that we never discussed how they felt about reading or writing. How they felt as literacy community members in our learning community. My students' opinions mattered on the surface, and yet, my actions and the tasks I dictated told them otherwise. Yes, we had choice in what we read, but not in what we did with it. And the program certainly did not help us uncover who we were as readers.

Then—When We Get Lost in Our To-Dos

Now I realize to be good at other things I have to be good at reading.
—Kendra, seventh grader

I did not realize just how little time 45 minutes was until I had to teach English language arts in only 45 minutes. Those first few weeks I meticulously planned every detail in order to try to teach as much as possible. I had the notion that independent reading time would fit in there somewhere, as would read-aloud, and then all of the projects we wanted to do. I wanted to do everything that I had done as a fifth grade teacher and somehow cram it into 45 minutes. Yet, after a few miserable weeks, I realized that there was no possible way to do it all, even if every minute was spent purposefully. I felt like a failure, because how was I supposed to create a passionate reading (and writing!) environment when I had no time to develop it? So things started to slip away from me; the first to go was the read-aloud; after all, that takes a lot of time, so it was an easy one to forego. Another was independent reading. Some days we would have it, other days we would not because of what we needed to get through. Conferring with students seemed like an impossible task, as did students choosing their own paths to learning. As often happens when we are faced with an overwhelming curriculum, I quickly started to focus more overall on what we needed to get through, rather than create a learning experience that my students would want to be a part of.

I am not alone; this "get-through-it" classroom experience is very common in our schools where we are creating efficient content machines at the expense of student joy. But I did not know what else to do. At the time, it felt like joy and an individual connection to the curriculum for each student was something I hoped to get to, not something I could necessarily fit into our lesson plans. Luckily for my first-year seventh grade students though, it did not take long before I saw the error of my ways. There was no possible way that I could go on just trying to get through as much as possible. These kids were not excited about coming to English class, and I was having a hard time keeping up my own enthusiasm level. Once again, I was confronted by a very simple truth; the lack of enthusiasm or engagement was not a sign of fault within my students, but rather a sign of fault within my own teaching. While there were factors outside of my control that definitely shaped our experience, such as the 45-minute time frame, and also that I was teaching all of the components of English and not just reading, it really came down to how I was shaping our experience together. As my husband told me many years ago when I thought I should quit teaching, "You can't change the kids, but you can change the way you teach." I realized that although I spoke of the importance of reading, most of my students were not reading, and that instead of developing as readers, we were stagnant. I knew then that I had to create non-negotiables for our learning experience that not only would guide the students but would guide me as I planned our lessons. Because if I did not make certain things non-negotiable, then we would not get to them. So in conversation with one of the incredible special education teachers at my school, Kelly, we figured out what we could not sacrifice in the quest to create a classroom experience where students had a chance to fall in love with reading. These components were nothing special by themselves but joined together they have transformed the learning experience my students have had and the teaching experience I get to have.

Now—The Most Important Elements of Our Learning Community

Kids would enjoy reading a lot more if they didn't have to write about the book they just read.

—Johnny, seventh grader

I woke up at 5 a.m. with my heart in my throat and my mind spinning, an experience shared by many teachers as we awake on the very first day of school. I did not wake up early just because I was excited, but rather because of my own nerves; would this be the year that no student would love reading? Would this be the year that they would revolt? Would I be able to find success as I had in years past? As I drove toward school, with the sunrise following me, I knew that my doubts would also follow me, not just throughout that day but probably for the next few months. After all, creating a passionate reading environment is not something that just happens overnight. It is hard work, it is intentional, and it is a commitment we must continually make even as some kids seem to fight us every step of the way. At the end of the day, after five English classes and an intervention class, my nerves had calmed somewhat. Seeds had been planted, and yet, I knew there was much work to be done. This is the reality for all teachers of reading; we plant seeds and hope that by the end of the year a transformation will have taken place. Sometimes a child is already a reader and we must nourish the growth, sometimes it comes down to the very last days of our year together, and sometimes the transformation does not happen until years after us, But whatever the case, we must approach each day with an incredible sense of urgency. We must fill our minds with the research we need to support our ways, and we must be passionate about the things we see as most important to further reading success—in my case, it means giving the students time to read within our short time together, finding a way to confer with each child, incorporating as much choice and freedom as possible, and doing meaningful work with our reading rather than "get-it-done" tasks. Inspired not only by the research of the experts whose books I read, but also by the truths that my students share with me, these components are what drive us toward the passionate reading learning community every lesson, every day, and every year. One that will transform not just the reading lives of our students this year, but also provide a foundation for years to come, no matter the instruction they receive.

Yet, the path that these components led me on is not an easy one. Creating an environment where students can flourish no matter what subject you teach is not something that just happens. While some teachers make it seem effortless, it is within this illusion that all of the hard work lies. If you were to visit our classroom those first few months, you would certainly see growth, but you might not notice all of the behind-the-scenes systems and decisions that are in place for this to function. Simply offering students choice in what they read is not enough; neither is giving them the time to read, nor having great books accessible. While these components may be enough for some, it will not be for all. There are therefore choices we have to make; we choose to have purposeful conversations and engage in meaningful work with texts. We choose to keep an ongoing dialogue about what works and what does not in our learning community. I choose to spend time conferring with my students, as well as spend hours outside of school reading children's literature. I choose to spend time looking for better ways to teach and reach my students and to continually self-reflect. This system is not perfect; this book was not written so others could "teach like Pernille." Instead, it is written as a way of showing you what these components can look like in an actual learning community filled with students who are on many different parts of their reading journey. It is because of these incredible students that I had to realize what to hold sacred, and the most sacred thing we have in our learning community will always be one we do not control—time.

Time and How Little of It We Have

Let your students read more, even for kids who don't like to read, they just need to find a good book.

—Delaney, seventh grader

My biggest ally in the quest to create passionate readers is time. The one thing we seem to have such precious small amounts of in the 45-minute class setup. The one thing we all wish we had more of for any of the subjects we teach. While I could pine over the 90-minute or longer literacy blocks I used to have as a fourth or fifth grade teacher, I have long ago realized that I need to make what I have work. That I need to embrace the 45-minute time frame as my ally, not my enemy, even if I still look for ways our master schedule can change. So every day the same thing happens as we start class; we have 10 minutes of independent, free-choice reading. Only 10, because our 45 minutes do not allow us more, but always 10 and always every day, unless something really big is in the way. This is my biggest investment, because let's face it, if we are indeed a class where reading is discussed, then reading also needs to take place in it.

If you were to enter our classroom during those 10 minutes, you might be shocked at how still it is. At how the quiet surrounds us as students are transported into other worlds. How when the timer beeps or I tell them good morning, calling students back, it is like time starts again from having stood still those first 10 minutes. It does not start that way in the beginning of the year. During that first week of school, I ask my students to bring a book to class with them because they will need it. Some kids bring a book, but many show up empty-handed and instead randomly grab a book off the shelf closest to them, giving it little thought. It seems that by seventh grade, a lot of our readers have gone into hiding. A lot of our readers have forgotten what a great book feels like. So a few days into the year, no later than the fourth day, I set the timer as the very first thing and I ask them to read for the full 10 minutes. Their reactions are varied. Kids jostle, a few start to read, others pick up a book and flip through it, pick up another book, flip through that. Whisper to their friend, check their phone, and anything else many of them can think of to not read. Simply put, many students, and yes, even the ones who excel at school, have mastered the art of nonreading by the time they become adolescents. As one student told me, "I use to fake read simply so I didn't have to try." I think we are all confronted by the myriad of reading personalities; those that groan when we tell them reading time is up to those who didn't even read a single word. We must create spaces within our learning communities for all of them. So as a new year gets started, I tell them about the gift of the 10 minutes. About how we will start every single day with reading. How they need to come to class with a book that they actually want to read. How this is my gift to them and I do expect them to read outside of class, but that every day, if I can help it, we will start with reading, and it is up to them to make it worthwhile. As I tell them to "Settle in, settle down, get to reading" they slowly fall into their books. Some need prompting, others needs practice, and others need me to get out of their way. Every day it is the same; settle in, settle down, get to reading, and so they do, some more slowly than others. Because the expectation is there, the opportunity is there, and I, as the teacher, am there to help, and so are all of their classmates.

There is no fanfare as we start our first 10 minutes of independent reading. There is no buildup. Instead, students enter and right as the bell rings, I tell them to please start reading. That first day of 10 minutes of independent reading is never one for the record book, and neither is the next, but throughout the repetitive nature of expecting the same thing every day, of holding them to high expectations day in and day out, of being patient with those who fight it, students slowly start to settle in quicker. To come to class prepared. To actually find or ask for a book that they may like rather than just grab something off the shelf. I stand back and watch, feeling out their habits, gently guiding those that need it, but mostly just watching those first few days, taking mental notes as I get to know this new flock of students. The kids that flip the pages aimlessly are a conversation waiting to happen. The kids that keep looking at the clock is another. The kids immersed deeply in their book that continue to read after the timer has gone off, well, they are also readers I need to get to know so that I can protect the connection they already feel to text. All of these kids and their reading habits are all conversations waiting to happen. I do not confer those first few days of reading—that typically starts around day seven or so—but instead just watch. Who are these kids I am now teaching and what do they look like when they are reading? There are clues all around me; the kids that showed up without a book, we quickly book shop together as I get to know how well they know their own reading preferences, the kids that aimlessly flip pages or just stare into space, a gentle tap on their shoulder or just a walk by usually gets them back on the pages, and those kids that are already into their books, those I leave alone. Those kids that every day, even in April, come to class with no book, well, every day I hand them a book to try, every day I ask. After the 10 minutes are up, I call them back to me, give them a minute to find their bearings (a good book will pull you away) and congratulate them. There are always things to compliment, even if only a few kids were reading. I also like to ask, "How many of you are reading a great book right now?" and watch for a show of hands. If there are children whose hands are not up, then I remind the class that life is too short to read bad books and encourage them to find another one. The idea of book abandonment being an acceptable part of being a reader is one that I want to encourage any chance I can get.

There are many benefits besides reading to starting our lesson with 10 minutes of independent reading time. I often have students called out of the room for various reasons, and so rather than wait for all students to be present to start a lesson, I know that they will usually show up within the 10 minutes and therefore not miss out on instruction, even if it hurts my heart to see them miss out on reading time. Students also enter the classroom at various emotional stages, so when children are able to start with a calming activity like reading, it allows them to self-regulate before they are asked to engage with others. While it also offers me an opportunity to confer with students, which will be discussed more in detail later, it also lends me an opportunity to merely check in on students' well-being. Anyone who has taught large numbers of students knows how long it can take to establish relationships with every student, so those 10 minutes allow me to do just that. Finally, we know that recess is vital for student learning, and yet in our middle school system recess is usually limited to lunch. That means that our students are asked to constantly be on, fully engaged, and prepared to learn in every single subject area they encounter, with only a few minutes passing time to reset their energy and brain. Having students start with reading in a comfortable spot is a form of mini-recess to many; a break from all of the demands of school, as long as the task itself does not add further stress (Murray and Ramstetter 2013).

Yet, the biggest reason why we start with 10 minutes of reading lies within reading itself. Simply put, the power of our 10 minutes of independent reading time cannot be disputed. In fact, research shows that even just adding 10 minutes of daily reading will dramatically increase a child's exposure to words ("Adding Ten Minutes of Reading Time Dramatically Changes Level of Print Exposure"). Why does that matter? Because more exposure to words means more background knowledge, and more background knowledge means easier comprehension, which will lead to reading being a less frustrating experience. So while I ask my students to read at least 20 minutes outside of class, I can only hope that they do so, but I can see to it that they read 10 minutes in class every day with me. And for some of my students, that makes all the difference. So while our 10 minutes may not seem like a lot, and for many it is not enough, it does plant a seed for further reading. We can utilize those 10 minutes to be an enticer of sorts, to get the children hooked into a story so that they will want to read later. This is why choice in text is so important; we want children to read a great book so that they will want to find the time to read more later.

Component of Change: Creating Pockets of Reading Time

When teachers give students time to read in school it is a chance for kids to enjoy a book in a safe, peaceful, and quiet place. It calms me down and I don't have to worry about any issues.

—Lily, seventh grader

Creating pockets of time for students to simply shut off the world and immerse themselves in text is important for many reasons, but one often overlooked is for the sake of sanity. Many of us teach in jam-packed schedules, in schools dictated by a bell, where students are expected to always attend, always be enthused, always be on. Giving students the gift of silent reading time with few curricular expectations is not just a way for them to become better readers, but also a way for them to take a break from the mania of the day. In his book, *Flow: The Psychology of Optimal Experience*, Mihaly Csikszentmihalyi describes how we feel when we reach a state of flow or reach "the zone." This state of full immersion characterized by feeling lost within the process and the world fading away is one that we can glimpse within our reading time in class. We know students have reached the zone during reading when every child is immersed in the book and the quiet feels like a delicious blanket enveloped around us. When students know what the expectations are, when students know themselves better as readers, when they know where they fit into our vision for our learning, they can start to focus on the story in front of them. They can immerse themselves until the world, indeed, fades away and all that is left is them and their imagination. No stress, hopefully. To read more about the power of the reading zone or reaching this state of flow, read *The Reading Zone* by Nancie Atwell, a landmark book in the support of quiet, uninterrupted reading time. So look for opportunities in your day to bring back reading, and let the students read without interruptions. Let them read where they would like in the room, let them read what they would like. Let them read not for the sake of an assignment but for the sake of falling into the pages of a book and staying there, even if only for a little bit. Finding time to read in class, therefore, is one of the most important steps, if not *the* most important step, toward creating passionate readers.

While I wish we could all find more time to add to our English block within our schedules, often that is not a possibility. What we are faced with instead is how to use the time we have more effectively, which often is easier said than done. I encourage anyone, no matter how many minutes you have for your instructional time, to really look at what you find to be your essentials. What are the most vital components of the experience that you are trying to create for and with your students? What are the non-negotiables in your day, and how will you protect them once they are discovered? For me, giving students time to read has been a cornerstone of our passionate literacy community because I believe it plants a seed for further reading. Kids who read with us, and read great books, tend to do more reading outside of our learning communities. Research agrees, as studies show that students who participate in silent sustained reading (SSR) read more both immediately and after they are no longer in SSR (Krashen 2016). Yet it is not just about the increase in reading; I have to see my students read so I can understand them as a reader. I need to have time to speak with them about their reading lives so that they can further explore the reading identity they have. That needs to happen within the classroom, on the foundation that we plant within our reading time, and not be based on work they maybe do outside of school.

So the very first step to creating time to read is finding the time. How much time can you give them? I do not recommend less than 10 minutes, as it sometimes take a few minutes for students to fall into their books. When in your block of time, can you offer students a chance to read? Which pockets will work every day? I have tried independent reading throughout our class time together, but keep coming back to having it in the beginning, as it settles the students in nicely. That way, too, it is never cut, nor do we run out of time. It also sends a message to the children that before we get into other work, we must do the most important thing—read a self-selected book. This message may not overtly register with children, but it certainly lets them know what we see as important.

A few questions to ask yourself can be:

◆ What is your time being spent on right now?
◆ What are your non-negotiables?
◆ Where is time being wasted?
◆ What will the daily routine be for your students to slip into reading—having a routine matters, as it will save a lot of time because the children already know what to do.
◆ What will you spend your time on as the students are reading?

Once you have found a pocket of time, consistency is key. Developing stronger readers is a fragile thing, one that requires a daily commitment to support the stage they are at. It doesn't happen if we only implement reading time once in a while. So rather than dedicate one day a week to reading, find time every day to make it a part of the expectation. My students know after the first week of school that they are expected to bring a book every single day, no exception. They also find out that they should like the book they are reading, a novel concept it seems, rather than just settle for an "ok" book. Indeed, if the book is right for them, they should want to keep on reading after the 10 minutes are up. This idea of only reading amazing books may seem novel; however, I repeatedly find students who are not reading great books or who would rank their books a "6" or a "7" on a 10 point scale thinking that this is the only type of book experience they will have and who therefore end up with little to no desire to read more. This pattern turns into a long-term affliction—settling for books that are okay rather than taking the time to search for books that are amazing. At some point, these children start to believe that all books are just okay and they dislike reading even more. While I wish that I could give my students a longer chunk of time rather than just the 10 minutes, in a way this short amount of time means that it is manageable even for the most stubborn of readers. As Stephen Krashen writes, "Rather than forcing reading, and possibly making it distasteful, small doses are much more likely to work" (Krashen 2004). Ten minutes can still seem like a small hill to climb, but it is a lot smaller than the mountain that 30 minutes on one day of the week can seem like, at least in the beginning.

Keeping it consistent includes:

- ◆ Setting expectations for what independent reading time looks like; include students in this conversation for true ownership.
- ◆ Communicating expectations at the beginning of the year and then whenever needed.
- ◆ Keeping yourself consistent. Are you expecting the same thing every day?
- ◆ Identifying needed differentiation for students. While some students will have no problem accomplishing 10 minutes of independent reading every single day with few prompts, others may need help with figuring out where to read and what to read, and can even be given smaller chunks of time to read in the beginning. Part of your job is to help each child discover where on the journey they are and to help them move forward.

The Five Tenets of Choice

Teachers should give students time to read in school every day because sometimes you can't do it at home. At school, you can get hooked on a book.

—Anni, seventh grader

Being a middle school teacher with the 45-minute time constraint means that as much as I wish I could teach reading and writing together in every single class, it is not always possible. So instead, my colleague Wendy and I have decided to frame our quarters in either a reading or writing lens. While neither is ever forgotten, depending on the quarter we do things in a more concentrated way. That means that for two quarters of the year, reading is our main focus, so we teach writing through a reading lens, which includes studying copious amounts of picture books to use them as mentor texts, developing our analysis skills by using *Notice & Note* by Kylene Beers and Bob Probst, and putting our newfound skills into written work, as well as developing our speaking skills through debates, book recommendations, and speeches on an array of topics. While two of our quarters have more of a writing lens, they are still heavily influenced by our reading, as students create nonfiction picture books for younger audiences around the world, write narratives exploring pacing and sequencing through studying picture books and other mentor texts, as well as "take breaks" by performing poetry or our favorite picture books. We are also standards based, meaning that I have seven core standards that I have to explore with my students and provide them opportunities to master. This means that we pick a few standards to work with every quarter, rather than all seven. This also means that since we are not product centered when it comes to assessment, we have freedom to make the curriculum fit our unique learners. (See appendix for our standards.) We may not have as much time to go as deep as we would like, but we certainly try to make the most of it. Framing our quarters within these lenses also allows me to not interrupt students during their 10 minutes of independent reading. I do not ask students to jot things down or put post-its into their books. Instead, I look for them to reach a state of full immersion in their text, uninterrupted by tasks. If I need students to practice a reading skill or work through lessons with their texts, I do a mini-lesson after they read and then ask them to return to their texts to practice. That way, they get reading time "just" for reading, as well as reading time to practice specific skills. For the students who continually struggle with finding a great book, I will often have a stack of picture books or a selection of short stories for them to use to practice the skill. (See https://pernillesripp.com/our-favorite-books/ for current and ongoing recommendations for picture books.)

While my colleagues and I enjoy immense trust and support from our administration as far as curricular decisions, we do work within the American public school system. We therefore have certain benchmarks and content areas we must explore with our students, which means that I am not always able to provide students with choices in the product they create. As someone who believes that the way to reengage students in learning is through choice, I have had to find a way to incorporate more choice throughout our curriculum, particularly when what we are doing is dictated by outside forces. This has therefore led to the creation and implementation of operating under the five tenets of choice at all times within our learning community. These five tenets are:

1   Choice in engagement, meaning how they access the learning. Do they need small group instruction or one-on-one conferring; are they independent, or do they want to work with a peer? I have students do a pre-assessment of how they would like to work through a project and then I plan my classes according to their needs. To see a sample pre-assessment survey, please see the appendix.

2   Choice in product, meaning what they would like to create to show their understanding and exploration of a concept. Sometimes this means full control of the product, depending on the standards we are working with, while other times it only means minimal choice, such as the format of their written work.

3   Choice in setting, meaning how and where they would like to learn. As discussed previously, students need to be afforded opportunities to manipulate the learning community environment to suit their needs. This is part of their learning journey, and so students can choose where they sit, how they sit, whether they work in the classroom or in other designated areas, as well as how they use the environment they are working in.

4   Choice in timeline, meaning when they are ready to be assessed. While this one is harder to do at times, I do try to provide flexible timelines for students, as well as stay attuned to what else is happening in other classes. This may mean that for a longer project, I will tell students what the final day is for them to turn something in, but that they can turn it in any time they are ready before then, or it may be that I ask them within a certain time period to show me mastery of a standard and they then choose the due date.

5   Choice in assessment, meaning how and what I assess as far as their mastery of concepts. Inspired by Kelly Gallagher, I will often ask students to turn in the piece that they think showcases their

depth of understanding the best and then assess and confer with them regarding this one piece of work. This allows students more flexibility and control over how they are assessed as well as gives them the opportunity to reflect on what mastery really means. This tenet also means that once students have shown mastery for a quarter, they do not have to prove it to me again, but can instead move on to more challenging work. This is a way for me to ensure that students are provided with learning that matches their needs better and also allows them for more self-directed learning.

While I may not always be able to provide students with choices within all of these tenets, I am able to provide them with choice in at least a few of them at all times. This allows students to be in control more of how they learn, and it has led to an increase in student engagement. Students want to be more invested when they feel that the teacher trusts them to make decisions that matter. To see more about this journey and how to further engage students, please see my book *Passionate Learners—How to Engage and Empower Our Students*.

Component of Change: Incorporating More Choice

Help your students want to be in your class by giving them choices.
—Kaitlyn, seventh grader

Asking my students how I could be a better teacher has fundamentally changed the way I teach. I, as an adult, take my freedom of adaptation of my learning for granted. I feel I have earned the right to certain privileges within my own learning journey and these rights, such as adapting the learning environment to fit my needs as much as possible, is one that furthers my own investment into the learning at hand. Once we reflect on our perceived rights as adult learners, it is only natural that we realize that the children we teach will also want to have as much choice as possible. Therefore, asking yourself how you can offer more choice within your perimeters is the first place to start.

A few questions to help you reflect are:

- How many choices are students given every day within your learning environment?
- How can students' ideas be incorporated more into your curriculum?

- ◆ If choice in product is not an option, than what other choices can students be given control over?
- ◆ How can students adapt the learning experience they have to still fit within the curriculum you are exploring?
- ◆ How will students be offered more responsibility for their own learning journey?
- ◆ How will choice be scaffolded for those students who may not be ready for ultimate freedom?
- ◆ What would you have loved as a child to be able to control more in your education?

Spending time reflecting on the impact of choice on student engagement is time well spent. And I have found that even within severely restricted curriculums, choices can still be offered to students. What matters is that we take the time to really dissect what we are being told to do and then find ways to regain control in the things we are not being told to do. I think we often assume that we have little control over much within our learning communities, yet there are always aspects that remain within our control; sometimes we just have to spend time uncovering them first. If the idea of handing back control to your students frightens you, start small. Perhaps you are not ready to give them full control over the product they create, but you can offer them a few choices such as which technology tool to use or who to work with. Start small and build on, with time you will often realize that your initial fears of more freedom turning into chaos were unfounded.

This being said, I also am aware of my own privilege. Many teachers are not as fortunate as I am; I do not have a purchased curriculum to follow in my English classes, but instead have been given the opportunity to create my own, as long as my colleague and I line up in which standards we explore within our quarters. We also have a common planning time when we swap ideas, decide on major units, and support each other when needed. While this format is liberating, it can also be quite intimidating at times, and yet I am grateful for the opportunity to truly create a curriculum that will serve the needs of the unique learners I have. While I re-use some explorations every year, there are always new ideas to try with the students, all based on what type of community we have established. However, if you are faced with a purchased curriculum or a created one that every teacher is expected to follow, I hope you have a chance to adapt it to fit your needs. In fact, if you are an administrator or somehow involved in curriculum purchasing decision, I hope part of your discussion centers on the point that we do not teach the same children as the program is based on. That our students may never share the same experiences as those kids who tested the curriculum and made it research-based, nor may they share the same background. This is important and should be remembered at all times because if a purchased curriculum or administrative decisions do not allow us to adapt it to our students, then it will never be as powerful as it needs to be. If we are chained to a curriculum map so we can all teach with fidelity based on other people's students, then we are not teaching the students in front of us.

So while there are many wonderful programs and curriculums for purchase, that are based upon solid research, I encourage you to also do the following three things:

Create an open dialogue. Teachers need to know that they can question the program and that they have a voice. There should be nothing too sacred for reflection and discussion in any district. Make sure that choosing a curriculum to purchase is not a top-down decision and that you constantly assess whether this program is what you need. Just because you spent money on something does not mean it is right for everyone. And just because you spent a lot of money on it at some point does not mean that it still works.

Allow teachers to modify, adapt, and change as needed. That doesn't mean compromising the program, but instead it means trusting teachers as the professionals they are to create an even better experience for their students. One that allows them to teach the very kids they are supposed to teach. That does not mean teachers are being subversive; it simply means that they are responding to gaps that they see and doing something about them. No program will ever be the perfect fit for all of our kids, all of our teachers, and all of our schools. They are vast road maps, not step-by-step directions.

Ask the students. If students are losing their love of reading, writing, science, math, or any program they are in, then we have a serious problem. It does not matter that the program may be the best for creating deep comprehension if students hate doing it, or if a program increases the number of books read but no child reads for the pleasure of it. If a curriculum program is creating robots in our learning community, then we should be worried. And we should take action, and we do that best by asking the students what is going on. Then we listen and then we change.

Whatever framework we work within—whether in 45-minute time blocks or longer ones, whether in a standards-based or a grade-based district, and whether we have total freedom or are scripted—there is a way to make the experience we create better for the students we teach. It may not be obvious and it may not be easy to do, but the first thing we can do is ask the students we teach whether what we are doing is working for them and then changing according to their truths. So if you find yourself in the situation where you can tell that something is not working for your students, speak up. Do it kindly, but do speak up, because administration cannot engage in a conversation that they do not know is needed. Ask your students, involve parents, and collect your evidence. Start a conversation before parameters you teach within become an educational barrier to success. Don't stay silent if you see something harming students. The change starts with us and our courage.

Dear Administrators

I have been pleading with teachers for a few years to please help students become passionate readers. I have given as many ideas as I could and directed toward the great minds that inspire me as well. I have begged at times, sharing the words of my students as proof that we teachers have an immense power when it comes to either nurturing a love of reading or killing it. There are so many things we teachers can do that will have a lasting effect.

And yet, it is not just the teachers that have an immense power over whether children will read or not. It turns out that much of that power also lies within the realm of administration. In fact, many of you are doing incredible things to create schools that are seen as literacy communities that cherish the act of reading and becoming readers. What are they doing? What can you do to foster a love of reading school-wide?

You can believe in choice for all. That means protecting the rights of students to read the books they choose. To help staff, support this as well by speaking about choice and making sure not to put restrictive policies in place that will hinder children from developing their own reading identity. That will stop children from choosing a book they want to read. Teachers should not be the only ones choosing books for students—please don't put them in that position. Instead, they should be working with students to learn how to self-select great books based on many things, not just their levels!

You can buy books. Research shows again and again how vital it is to students becoming better readers to have not only a well-stocked school library, but also a full classroom library. Students need books at their fingertips, not far away, and they need high-quality, high-interest books. That takes money. Please help out in any way you can.

You can fight to have a librarian full-time in your building. Everywhere we are seeing libraries that have no librarians, yet a knowledgeable librarian can be the lifeblood of a reading community. I know budgets are being slashed, but the librarian should be seen as a necessity in schools, not as a frivolous privilege.

You can celebrate books read. Not the number of minutes logged or the points gained in computer-based reading programs. How about keeping a running tally of how many books students self-selected to read and then finished? How about keeping a display board of all of the picture books being shared in your school, yes, even in middle school and high school? How about showcasing all of the favorite books that your school community has read as visitors enter your school? Celebrate the right things, not the ones that can kill a love of reading.

You can protect the read-aloud. When schedules are made, there should be time placed in for reading aloud. This should not be seen as a frill, or as something that would be nice to fit in if only we had more time. All students at every age should encounter an adult who reads fluently with expression aloud to them every day. It develops their minds as readers and creates community. This should not just be reserved for special times in elementary school, but should be protected throughout a child's reading experience in school. Our students need to hear text read aloud to model their own fluency, to have a deep reading experience, to be exposed to text they may not otherwise reach for, and to also have a bond with the rest of their peers. Embracing the read-aloud, whether picture book or chapter, means that we embrace all of the benefits that come with reading aloud, which was called the "single most important thing we could do for building the knowledge required for future success in reading" (Nation of Readers).

You can promote independent reading time. Students reading silently is not time wasted; it is one of the most important investments we can make in our school day for any child, any age. If you want children to become better readers, then give them the time to read.

You can hire teachers that love reading. I am amazed that there are teachers who teach literacy in any capacity that do not identify themselves as readers. This should not be happening. Years of experience show that students will read more if we read as well and are able to create a book community where our love of reading is a cornerstone of what we do. Even when I taught non-literacy subjects, even when I taught science, the fact that I read for my own pleasure meant that our conversations were deeper and more engaging, and that the students trusted me as a reading role model.

You can have tough conversations. Part of my job as a teacher is to grow and learn, and while I think that most of my ideas are solid, I wish an administrator would have questioned me when I had students do reading logs and forced book reports a few years back. While the pushback may be hard to swallow, it certainly would have made me think. However, within those tough conversations, please do listen to the teacher as well. What are they basing their decisions on? Perhaps they are the ones who are right; perhaps not, but ask the questions and keep the bigger goal in mind—students who like to read!

What else can you do to create a school where the love of reading flourishes?

You can be a guest read alouder.

You can have books in your office for students to read.

You can share your own reading life by displaying your titles outside your office.

You can make assemblies and other fun events celebrate literacy.

You can bring in authors.

You can promote reading literacy projects like the Global Read Aloud or Dot Day.

You can ask students what they are reading whenever you see them.

You can institute school-wide independent reading time.

You can stand up for poor literacy decisions being made within your district.

You can ask your teachers for ideas. You can ask your students what they need and then implement their wishes when possible.

You can send your teachers to professional development with the likes of Kylene Beers, Donalyn Miller, Penny Kittle, Kelly Gallagher, and any other of the incredibly talented literacy experts that inspire us all.

There are so many things that fall within your realm. Please help us teachers (like my principal Shannon Anderson does) protect the love of reading that students have and nurture it as we teach. You can choose to create passionate reading environments or you can support decisions that smother them. The choice is yours.

The Investment of a Reading Check-In Conference

I think when she [the teacher] comes around and sits down to see how we've been doing with reading shows that she wants to get to know us better as a reader.
—Alex, seventh grader

Another major benefit to starting class with 10 minutes of reading is that I get to confer and do a reading life check-in with a few readers every day. Using those first minutes to speak to my students about themselves as readers has led me to realize that while I cannot do an actual mini-lesson in those few minutes, I can gather information and focus on their reading identity during that time. I therefore use the time to gather clues for what types of mini-lessons I need to create for small groups. A great book to read for mini-lesson ideas is *The Reading Strategy Book* by Jennifer Serravallo. There are, however, exceptions to the rule if I uncover a particular, dire situation. I then take the full 10 minutes to help them directly. Particularly in the beginning of the year, reading conferences often morph into supported book shopping with a student as I uncover that they don't really know how to select a book or do not like the book they are pretending to read. However, as the year progresses, the goal is for them to be able to independently book shop and select a text at least to try. Within the 10 minutes, though, I typically can get to three students. I come to the students, equipped with my binder and pen, ready to ask them questions. By me moving instead of them, we save time and they can get as much reading time as possible until we meet. Then I just need one question to start every conference, "What are you working on as a reader?" The direction of the conference then is directed by their answer and may involve goal setting, book discussions, or simply what their reading experience is at the moment. I love that the students determine the path of the conversation, and I adapt our short time together to fit their needs.

I use a simple system to keep track of my notes (please see appendix for an example sheet), and it changes based on needs. I used to take a lot of notes during my conferring, but now I find the need just for three different things: my observations, their answers, and what now. Every student, therefore, has a sheet with three different conferring boxes on it; each class has its own 1-inch binder for me to keep track; and I write down only what I need to better teach the child. That means I am working on writing down only the essentials, in the moment, and still trying to think of what to help him or her with. This has gotten easier, of course, as I have had more experience teaching and am exposed to more student conversation. Yet with every new batch of students, it always takes me a while to have really great reading check-ins. I am at peace with that, because I am getting to know the students through every conversation. I also ask students how I can best support them; some students will have excellent ideas, while others are unsure. This follow-up question provides me with a glimpse into their reading identity. Do they even know what they need to work on, or are they unsure? Incorporating conferring within the students' 10-minute reading block means that I am fully attentive to what the students are saying and not thinking of other things. The short note-taking sheet means that I am more focused on what I write down, as well as what we need to work on next. The students seem to like it because they are getting more attention and still getting reading time. And the things I have uncovered? They are things I would not typically have uncovered no matter how many reflections I had students do, no matter how many small group lessons I would have conducted.

Component of Change: Reading Check-In Conference

I think a teacher can help me as a reader if the teacher seems interested in what I am reading, what genres I like and questions related to that.

—Kimberly, seventh grader

I think the biggest barrier to implementing reading check-ins or conferences is that when we are pressed for time, we may not see the short amount of time we can give to one-on-one instruction as enough. This fear of it not fulfilling the goals we have for communication with students should not hold us back though, for I have found that even the smallest amounts of time can add up to an incredible investment in our students. So the first step for starting today is truly just to start. Plan a lesson with students in which they can discuss what their reading goals are (see the next chapter for more discussion of this), and then tell them to record it somewhere—we record them right in our self-made reader's notebooks. Then pick a day, set up your binder or whichever system you prefer, and as they read independently start from the beginning of the alphabet and sit down next to a student and ask what he or she is working on as a reader. Do not get caught up in whether your documentation system is perfect, mine is tweaked all of the time; do not get caught up in whether you are writing the right things down, or even whether you are asking the right questions. No matter how much we plan, the students will almost always lead us in a direction we had not envisioned. Instead, be prepared to listen, be prepared to ask follow-up questions. "Tell me more about that," as author and literacy consultant Elin Keene would say. If you have an idea for something they can try, share it; if you don't, allow yourself to think about it. I think that often we, as teachers, believe we must have every answer to everything a child throws at us, yet this simply isn't possible. So if you are not sure how to help children on their reading journey, turn to others for help; colleagues both virtual and in-person, professional books, professional networks like NCTE or The Educator Collaborative, administration, or the kids themselves.

What to do with the information you gather may be your next question. I have found that I mostly use it in direct contact with students or if I am planning a small group lesson. I have long ago abandoned relying on my memory for who needs which skills taught or retaught, especially once I started to teach more than twenty-five students. So instead, I often write down a skill that might be beneficial to them as I plan my next small group lessons right on their sheet. That way I can quickly flip through my binder and find the kids that might have the same needs. Small group lessons are then given as the rest of the class work independently.

I have to remind myself that a check-in is just that, a quick moment to see how they are doing. And also that every reader, every child, deserves one-on-one time with the teacher. I have students that dread these check-ins, that hurry through them to get me to stop speaking to them, but I still return when their names are next. I also have students who might be strong readers and whom we might think do not need us, but trust me, they need us as well. Often our most established readers are our most undertaught. It is not meant to be a long one-on-one reading conference, because I would never get to any of the teaching that has to occur, and while I wish I could sit down with every single child for long periods of time, that is not the reality of the teaching parameters I face. Instead, I am grateful for the small conversations that we are able to have throughout the lesson as we get to know each other better and continue on our reading journey.

So while the 45 minutes of English class will never be ideal, will never be enough, will never feel like I can provide each child with the type of learning experience he or she deserves, it cannot hold us back. It cannot hold me back. While we may feel like time is the last thing we can give students, it is actually the first place we start. While we may feel like we have little control over the curricular decisions being made, we can still adapt to the parameters we are given. While we cannot always provide free choice for all children, we can provide them with choice in other aspects of their learning experience. After all, if we say to students that reading is the most important thing they can do to become better well-rounded adults, then we have to create an experience where students will understand the importance of being a reader.

Questions to ponder as you reflect on the foundations of your reading program:

◆ How would an outsider describe your reading program?
◆ How much time do students get to read every single day?
◆ What are the reading conversations that shape your reading learning community?
◆ How are student reading identities honored and supported?
◆ How can you tweak your existing program to become more student-centered?
◆ What courageous conversations might you need to have with administration when it comes to implementing new ideas or removing programs that harm the love of reading?
◆ What further reading or support do you need to further your own understanding of best reading practices?

The Reading Rules We Would Never Follow as Adults

Choice. The number one thing all the students I have polled through the years want the most when it comes to reading. No matter how I phrase the question, this answer in all of its versions is always at the top. Sometimes pleading, sometimes demanding, sometimes just stated as a matter of fact; please let us choose the books we want to read.

Yet, how often is this a reality for the students we teach? How often, in our eagerness to be great teachers, do we remove or disallow the very things students yearn for to have meaningful literacy experiences? How many of the things we do to students would we never put up with ourselves? In our quest to create lifelong readers, we seem to be missing some basic truths about what makes a reader. So what are the rules we would probably not always follow ourselves?

Removing choice. I have to start with the most obvious—removing choice in reading (and even in writing). We know that choice matters; we know as adult readers we revel in the sheer experience of being able to choose what we want to read. We take it for granted and will even rebel in small ways when someone says we have to read something. Choice is the cornerstone of our own literacy life, yet it is one of the first things we tend to remove for children, especially fragile or developing readers. And I get it, we think we know better when students repeatedly choose wrong, yet it is in the selection process that students can uncover who they are as readers, if we give them time to discuss, reflect, and yes, even try the things they choose that may not be a great fit.

Forced reflection. We seem to be reflecting kids to death with our requirements to write a little bit about every book they read. Or having them keep a reading journal or having them write about the signposts or whatever else they are finding when they independently read. It is not that we shouldn't have students reflect when they read, it is that we make these one-size-fits-all requirements where students cannot discover how they would like to digest their reading. How often do we as adults write a paragraph every time we finish a book? Or summarize it? Or make a diorama (which yes, I made my students do)? While I know adults who would love to do all of those things, I also know many who would not. In fact, many adult readers I know would slow down their reading or hide their reading if they had to do all of that "work." When I teach the signposts (from the excellent book *Notice & Note*), I tell my students that they are not expected to find them when they are reading at home, but that they are meant to be able to find them when asked. There is a big difference in the way they feel about the task because it is not something they have to do all of the time.

Forced tracking. Oh, reading logs, I am looking at you here. Yes, as an adult I track my reading on my Goodreads account. I even write reviews sometimes. But I don't track my pages (unless I have a bigger purpose in mind and then it is for a short amount of time), or time how long I read for, or even have my husband sign for me. I make time to read because I love reading. And while we can say that reading logs foster more reading because it is a checkup system, it also kills reading for many. If you want to see if the kids are reading, have them read in class and pay attention to what they are reading. Allow students to track in a way that is meaningful to them: Goodreads, notebook page, poster, pictures of books on their phone, or even through conversations. There is no one system that fits all, and if a system we have in place is even killing the love of reading for one child, then we need to rethink it.

Points and competition. Yes, Accelerated Reader, you have it coming. Plus, all of the other initiatives that we put in place to urge students to read. And I get it—we desperately want students to become readers and to keep reading, yet this short-term solution can actually have a long-term consequence; kids who do not read for reading's sake but for the prizes or honors attached to it. We know that there is minimal support for an increase in reading attached to rewards; in fact, it is mostly when students are given another book as a reward that it positively impacts their reading habits (Gambrell and Marinak). Yet even though we know what the research says regarding motivation and reading and how it can actually have adverse effects, we still continue to concoct programs to try to get them reading. How many adults, though, would read more because we then could take a computerized test that would give us points? How many adults would be okay with their reading lives on display for the world to see? Some would, while others would hate for the world to know something that they see as a personal discovery. Why do we assume that what might work for one child will work for all?

Limited abandonment. As an adult reader, I practice wild book abandonment, passing books on when I know they are not right for me, yet as teachers, we often have rules for when students are allowed to abandon a book. I used to subscribe to the 50-page rule myself. Why? If children want to abandon a book, they are on their way to knowing themselves better as readers. This is something to celebrate, not something to limit. If children are a serial book abandoners, and yes, I have a few of those, then we should be asking them why, rather than just stopping them. What did they not like about this book? What do they need to look for instead? Help them explore their reading identity so that they can develop it, rather than have them mimic yours.

Inane book shopping rules. My students used to be allowed to book shop on Fridays. That was it. Yet, as an adult reader, I book shop all of the time. I am constantly on the prowl for the next great read, and my to-be-read list is ever expanding. I get that book shopping or browsing sometimes becomes an escape for a child when he or she does not want to read, but then we work with that one child, rather than impose limits for all. My students know that book shopping can happen anytime during our independent reading time, or even if they have completed other tasks. I prefer that children want to look at books, rather than abhor it.

When my students started telling me their reading truths, I drove home in shame; how many of the things they told me had killed their love of reading were things that I had done myself as a teacher? How many of the things was I still doing? Yet, within the words of my students, I found the biggest truth of all—different children need different reading experiences. So now I try to create a passionate reading environment, where there is room and the needed scaffolds for all of my readers—not just those who can work in one system concocted by me. I know that sometimes large things are out of our control, yet there are so many small things that are under our control. Think of what made you a reader or what stopped you from becoming one, and then use that reflection to shape the way reading is taught and practiced in your own learning environment. Being a teacher means that we learn from our mistakes. I have made many, and it means that I continue to strive for better. We cannot do that if we don't listen to the students. And, you know what? Don't take my word for it—ask your own students. Then listen. Then do something about it.

5

Developing Student Reading Identity by Making Reading a Personal Journey

I believe a good book has to be great to you. It doesn't
matter what others think, just do what makes you happy.
—Bree, seventh grader

Before school starts, my school, Oregon Middle School in Oregon, Wisconsin, does two days of locker drop off, giving students a chance to bring their supplies in, try their new lock, and even poke around the building. My first year there, I was at work in my classroom on the first day of this event. The books were all meticulously displayed. Brand new picture books lined our whiteboards. The beanbags were fluffed and ready. Every bin had a specific and hopefully enticing book faced out. My reading poster for the summer was up, and I could not wait to see the reaction of my incoming students. Surely, they would be excited when they saw all of the books waiting for them. Surely, they would be eagerly asking to read the books.

A mother followed by her son came into the room, and they introduced themselves. He was one of my future students, and so I eagerly shook his hand and asked him if he liked to read. As soon as the words left my mouth, his facial expression changed to one of pure disgust. He looked me straight in the eye and said, "I don't read . . . thanks," as if I had offered him a particularly disgusting food item. His mother looked at me and then added, "Yeah, he has not read much the last few years, we are not quite sure what to do." I plastered a big smile on my face and told her we would work on it together. He did not seem impressed by my eagerness and asked if they could go now. They left, and my heart dropped; what had I gotten myself into?

I left that day wondering once again why I had moved from the incredible oasis that is fifth grade to this new reality of seventh. What on earth had possessed me to think that I had any chance in reaching seventh graders? That I knew anything about getting 12-year-olds to read? There were days during my first year with these older students that I cried. Feeling so lost in my mission to make kids like school and books again. There were days where I felt like I failed, that everything I did made little difference, and that surely one of these days those kids I taught would call me out as the fraud that I felt like. But they did not. Instead, they seemed to rally around me, around us, as we figured out how to make English a better class for them. As we figured out who we were together, who they were as individuals, and how their new identities could involve being readers. I felt the urgency every day to make school better, as do so many of my colleagues, to make reading something worth doing, worth falling in love with. I still do. Even if kids still tell me that they don't do reading, and good luck convincing them otherwise.

At the end of my first year, I had not changed that boy and his dislike of reading. There was no grand transformation or success story where all of a sudden he read every single night. That boy, he read once in a while. He abandoned books, still. He had a million excuses for why he did not have a book, but not always. There were others who had been transformed, but he had resisted until the very end. It happens in all of our learning communities. Teaching would be so much easier if we could see the influence that the learning may have on a child, but most of the time we do not. We can only plant the seeds that hopefully will grow into something bigger than even we could imagine. So we cannot expect miracles every day, even if we hope for them, even if we work for them. Because if we do, we will only see ourselves as failures. As though we cannot teach well. Instead, we must hope for small changes that will someday lead to a big transformation, even if that transformation happens long after they leave us.

So one day the next year when he stopped me in the hallway, I would never have guessed the reason why. "Hey, Mrs. Ripp . . . have you read *Gym Candy*? It's kind of mature, but I really like it. The librarian found it for me. You should read it." I stood there not quite believing what my ears had just heard. He recommended a book to me. Not because I asked him to. Not because I was his teacher. But because he was discovering that perhaps he could be a reader after all. That perhaps there were books for him. And perhaps, his old English teacher would like to hear about it. I walked away with a big smile on my face and a new book to add to my to-be-read pile.

So whenever a child tells me they do not read, that books are not for them, that they hate reading, I always think of the little change that perhaps I can help inspire. Of the small steps we can take together. Of how we may not see the transformation, but that if we make loving reading an urgent endeavor then perhaps we are planting a seed. And one day, maybe years later, that child will not feel like saying "I don't read . . . thanks" but instead will recommend a book to you. But that will only happen if we purposefully create the conditions for this shift in identity. If we purposefully create a community where all children can be supported and challenged in their reading journey. Where all children will find a personal reason to read, will experience how reading can change them, and will also know that they are not alone in this quest. Therefore, creating conditions in which students can uncover their reading identity, so they can strengthen and further it, is vital as we try to create passionate readers.

Then—Reading Is for Practicing Strategies, Not for Developing Their Reading Identities

At the beginning of the year, I hated reading. I used to doze off and stare into space. I would never read in independent reading, just sit there for the 45 minute class period. I would also read super slow when I did read because my mind was telling me I didn't want to read. When I read now, I actually read. I can also read for a longer period of time. One time I even found myself picking up a book in my free time.

—Mara, seventh grader

I do not recall a teacher ever asking me what I liked to read. I am sure it happened but clearly not on a regular basis, and I admit that for many years I did not ask my students about it often either. In our reading conversations, I focused on teaching reading, which to me meant comprehension strategies and reading practice, not exploration of who the children were as readers and who they would like to become. I used a whole-class novel, worksheet packets created by others, and predetermined book clubs led by me to make sure I could properly guide and assess their comprehension. I knew that my job as their teacher was to fully understand them as readers and so to me that meant that I had to also know the very book that they were demonstrating their knowledge in or their answers would not be valid. The first few years of my reading instruction therefore included carefully prepared lists of comprehension questions, as well as already planned conference goals. When I met with students, I led the conference with students answering most of my questions while I spent a lot of time taking notes. My conferences therefore often lasted at least 15 minutes per child. Conferences took a familiar path; the first week of school, we primarily discussed their reading history, who they were as readers, and how their summer reading had gone, and as the year progressed we spoke of the skills that were taught in our mini-lessons. It was exhausting to keep up with all of the notes and to try to plan for conversations that had not happened yet. It also left little room for following a different path for each child and focused much too much on skills, not experiences. While skills are incredibly important for a child to progress through reading, I no longer believe that it is *the* most important thing; a desire to read is. After all, it will not matter if we have taught every skill needed to a child to become a successful reader if he or she then decides to never read another book again.

Now I realize that a child knowing his or her likes and dislikes can tell us much about that child as a reader. If they have a list of books they love or books they cannot wait to read someday, I know they are on their way to cementing their identity as readers and will need support to stay on the path. On the other hand, if children instead answer in general terms when asked about their reading preferences, then I know that they do not know who they are as readers yet, and this year therefore becomes an opportunity to explore their identity. Even a child who speaks positively about reading and yet does not have much of a reading preference is not cemented in an identity as someone who reads, and must therefore still be handled with care. In fact, I would say that all readers need to be handled with care; after all, we can do a lot of damage in one year with a child. I know I did at times.

The conversations we have shape the readers that students become. Knowing that who they are as readers includes more than just the skills they still need to be taught is a vital step in teaching the whole child. Much as we must know our own reading identity in order to foster a passionate reading environment, we must therefore also provide ongoing opportunities for our students to discover and explore their own. Otherwise, much of the reading instruction we do will have less of a lasting effect. So what are we discussing in our learning communities? Are we discussing great books? Habits we are trying to form? How we book shop? How we abandon books? How they view themselves as readers? Or are we merely going through the checklists of our literacy curriculum in order to cover the content? Is the 45-minute time crunch, or whatever amount of time that we are given to teach reading, becoming the crutch that holds us back from really creating passionate reading environments? Because a passionate reading environment will not arise if we do not purposefully aim to create one. It does not matter how great of a literacy program you teach if you do not start a larger reading conversation with students. Because there is a difference between covering content and teaching students, we must take what we have to teach and infuse it with our love of literacy, but that becomes a choice we need to make.

As I changed my instruction and the experience I wanted to create in our classroom, I tweaked ideas and requirements all throughout our reading experience. While some of these changes will be discussed more in depth in a little while, here is an overview of the major changes that have framed our work for the past several years.

Then: I Will Tell You What to Read

I forced them to read certain books because I knew better. Armed with levels and lessons, I forced many children into giving up the book they were certain to struggle through and handed them a better-suited one. Better suited based on levels, reading abilities, but typically not interest.

Now: Please Choose Your Book

Students have free choice to read with few restrictions. Throughout the year, they have to read twenty-five books, fifteen of which must be chapter books. If a child is continuously abandoning books, we discuss, adjust, and try new things. We also spend time selecting books together and work on strategies to get through books that may be a bit out of the comfort zone.

Questions That Led Me to Change

Are students reading because they want to or because I told them to? Can students find books they want to read? Am I teaching to the future of this child or merely covering curriculum?

Then: Log It or Else . . .

Students had to prove they had read through either worksheets or a reading log. I used both reading logs and worksheet packets to look for proof of comprehension and certainly also proof of reading itself. Had children not completed their work, they were either excluded from an enticing experience such as a pizza party, or they would be kept in from recess. The questions asked on the worksheets were often surface level rather than deep thinking about their texts, and we did not have a lot of discussion in class. Summarizing each book they read was also a favored way of checking their reading, as I was more concerned about them proving they had read than what they were doing with their reading.

Now: Speak About Your Books

Students prove to me that they are reading in a myriad of ways without a reading log or a worksheet, the most common one being conversation. We discuss books frequently in class, and I have realized that there are so many ways we can see whether a child is reading, we just have to tap into it. One of the ways I know my students are reading is by watching their reaction when we start our reading time. Do they start right away and eagerly dive in; do they start before the bell even rings? Do they have to be reminded repeatedly to read; do they not even open their books? Kids who slowly get their book opened, who distract others on the way—those are the kids I need to check in with and help. How do you know your students are reading?

Questions That Led Me to Change

Are my reading practices doing long-term damage? Should the emphasis of our reading experience be on proving it or developing their love of reading? What is a reading log really telling me?

Then: Whole-Class Book, Whole-Class Discussion

We did the whole-class book throughout the year. This was to make sure we had a common text to discuss with which I could tie in comprehension questions. This also meant I really only had to know the few texts we did together, rather than read widely myself. Most instruction was facilitated by me through pre-planned activities and discussion questions. All students had to reach the same point of understanding and there was little room for individual creativity or thought.

Now: Whole-Class Read-Aloud

Rather than a whole-class novel coupled with work packets, we do the whole-class read-aloud. Using chapter books or picture books, we read aloud together as often as we can. Students can develop their discussion skills around a shared text, and I have a text to use when needed as a springboard. Students are then still free to read whichever book they want and apply our strategies discussed to that one once the read-aloud portion of the day is complete.

Questions That Led Me to Change

Do I have to do the whole-class novel? How else can we have deep reading conversations without the forced novel? Is this practice killing my students' love of reading? What type of reading experience does the whole-class novel truly create for my students? What am I trying to accomplish through the whole-class novel and can that be accomplished in a different way that will allow for choice?

Then: Stop and Post-It

All students had to use post-its and jot down their thoughts frequently as they read. This was a way for me to see their thinking while they read and check their application of reading lessons; I would even have them hand them in so I could assess them. Students were encouraged to stop and jot their thoughts every few pages as proof of their thinking while they read.

Now: Providing Uninterrupted Reading Time

For a few years, my students have asked me to please not interrupt their reading time, especially because they get so little of it. Now when I need to see student thinking, we have extra reading time in class and students then show me their thinking however they want. Some still use post-its, which I have readily available, others their notebook, or any other way they can think of. What matters is that they are finding a way for them to stop and think and then jot down their thoughts so that we can have some deep discussions. That way they know that in that moment they are practicing their reading skills by thinking about their reading and writing something down, but that cannot be all of the time. Students need time to read without interruptions.

Questions That Led Me to Change

Is the focus becoming more on post-its than deep reading? Do they ever have uninterrupted reading time, or are there always interruptions or things to do? What do students do with their writing about reading? Is it stopping them from liking reading? How else can they practice the skills I am teaching?

Then: Pre-Selected Texts with Pre-Made Questions

I always had an independent text to use for every small group. I always did guided reading with the same kids every week, and we always had either a pre-selected book club book or a text that I had selected. This way I could control the strategies we developed because I had pre-read everything and could thus lead the conversation. Students answered questions, but no real discussion ensued. Texts often came from purchased text sets and were all leveled with a teacher guide.

Now: Picture Books and Questions to Start Us Out

Sometimes I have a text, but more likely I have a picture book. Students and I read the text together and then work our way through it. All ages love picture books, and I have spent a lot of money getting great ones into the hands of my students. We read the book and then apply the strategy to their own book right then and there so that I can see whether they fully understand it. While I select the text with a strategy or question in mind, such as what is the theme, I have also learned to adapt our conversation along the way. If a group surprises me in their conversation, the format allows us to pursue the direction we need rather than stick to the plan that may not fulfill the needs of the group. If children need extra time, I hold them back while I release the others.

Questions That Led Me to Change

Am I thinking deeply about the texts that I am selecting to use with students or just choosing something based on an outside recommendation? Is there room for discussion and exploration of a relevant topic? Why does preparing for this take so much time—is that time that could be spent in a different way? Do students have a chance of directing the conversation? Who does most of the work in these small groups?

Then: Groupings Based on Levels

Groups were created based on level, artificially created through a computerized test or a reading inventory. I did not look at pace, interest, or specific skills needed, only what level the child was at. Children were therefore sometimes mismatched as they worked on the same skills, because the level was either inaccurate or they read at an entirely different pace than others did.

Now: Groupings Based on Need

Students are grouped based on needs. Typically, students go in and out of small groups that crop up throughout a week based on how they are doing on certain skills. This means that students don't feel labeled as being a "bad" reader because they are not in the same group day after day. They instead see that we are helping them with the skill they need and then released once they have it. I also set up opportunities for students to self-select whether they need a skill or not. So I might tell the class that today's small group will be on how to support your main idea with evidence and then tell them to meet me at a certain table. I then teach the students that feel they need the skill. If I know a child needs reteaching or further support in a particular skill, and they do not come over, then I pull together another group the following day with them included.

Questions That Led Me to Change

Are these groups valuable for the children selected to participate in them? Is there room for children to self-select the skills they feel they need? Do students know which skills they need to be successful readers? Do they feel respected in their choices?

Then: Teacher-Led Book Clubs

Students did book clubs with me as the guide. This type of guided reading was something I worked very hard at but frankly, it was exhausting. I always had to read ahead and prepare the discussions so that I could lead the conversations. Often I had a hard time keeping the six different books I was using straight, and trying to find multiple texts centered around the same theme was also hard. Students did little discussion beyond the surface of the questions I had prepared, but at least they had a shared reading experience.

Now: Student-Led Book Clubs

Students run the book clubs. I check in and help them push their thinking but they set the pace, they select the books based on group conversations, and they "manage" the club. I have to step in once in a while to help a student who is not adhering to the group's etiquette, but mostly the students are in control. They run their own discussions, I listen in and coach from the side, and they also decide what to do with the book after they have finished their reading. To see more details about the way we do our book clubs, see https://pernillesripp. com/2017/04/10/ideas-for-how-to-do-better-book-clubs-in-middle-school/

Questions That Led Me to Change

Are students invested in their book clubs? Who chooses the groups? Who chooses the books? Are students in control of what they are discussing? Does this mimic a "real-life" book club like adults would participate in?

There are so many things we choose to do within our reading instruction, or any instruction for that matter, that we think will help students, but we end up robbing them of the spark that carries them forward as readers. Although some of these things may work for other teachers, they have not worked for me, nor for many of my students. I am just grateful that my students have had the courage to tell me these things, but they would not have done so if I hadn't asked. So please, if nothing else, ask your students what helps them become better readers and then do more of that.

Now—Creating an Environment Where a Positive Student Reading Identity Is Explored and Solidified

When I come to English I'm always looking forward to reading. Reading to me is an escape from all the chaos and stress from school and, well, sometimes the world. Books take you on crazy adventures or wonderful fairy tales. Books make the impossible possible. Books make you happy, sad, and even mad. Books are amazing and every student should get a chance to read every day.

—Anna, seventh grader

I remember many of my first days of teaching throughout the years. For the first few years, the first day of school meant rules, putting away supplies, and laying the groundwork for what would be *my learning community*. We did not read, we did not have time for that; instead, we did some ice breakers and other planned activities. I was at the helm of the ship, so to speak, and students left with a pretty good idea of who was in charge. That changed, though, as I changed the way I taught, and now the first day of school feels a lot different. On the first day of school, I do not want to do activities. I do not want to play games. Nor do I want to fake my enthusiasm.

On the first day of school, I do not want to force student into awkward icebreakers, while they hope the teacher will forget it is their turn next. I will not force them to bare their soul or to share their dreams. Not yet, they are not ready. On the first day of school, we will not have many things planned. We will not spend precious time listening to me drone on. We will not run around hectically trying to figure it all out. Instead, on the first day of school, we will sit quietly and listen to a book read aloud. A picture book that the students have chosen from a pile of great books and then we will have time to speak to one another. We will cautiously start to feel each other out, find our friends, glance at the new people, and probably worry about the teacher. We will ask the questions about seventh grade that we have, not because we have to but because we will take the time if needed. Students will set the expectations of the learning community, as always, and it will take as much time as it needs. On the first day of school, students will be asked to always bring a book, to be ready to read, and to be ready to have a voice.

The first day of school is meant to be a great experience, but that does not mean we cram it full of things to do. That does not mean that we put on our entertainer hat and try to juggle as many balls as we possibly can. Instead, it means that we take the first step to get to know these students that have been thrust into our lives. That they take the first step in trusting us and trusting the community. That can only happen in a genuine way if we take things slowly. If we allow time to just be, to just sit, to just talk. So as you plan for the first day of school, plan for the quiet, for the reflection, for the conversation. Do not spend so much time planning for all of the things. Because this is not about how to prove how fun you will be this year, it is about showing the kids that you care and that within your learning community they will be readers. So on that first day, we plant the seeds for that. We lay the foundation for the type of experience we hope to have with all of the students, one in which they explore their own reading (and writing) identity in order to develop and strengthen it.

So, in order to start this conversation about student reader identity, I start our literacy year out by giving my students a separate reading survey in an effort to get to know them better. (See the appendix for a sample survey.) I ask for their honest answers, explaining that I know I have not earned their trust this early on but that I hope they will answer me honestly, as that is the only way I can get to know their true selves. Most students oblige and share their habits without hesitation; others need more time. Year after year, students have shared their reasons for why they may have fallen out of love with reading, and year after year, I have reflected on how many of those very things they report as deterrents are things that I have made students do myself because of well-meaning intentions. In fact, herein lies one of our biggest problems as teachers, we mean well with so much of our reading instruction and yet some of the things we are doing are complicit in the killing of the love of reading. We know what leads students to love reading. Richard Allington, renowned literacy researcher and educator, and many other researchers have given us the knowledge to create reading environments that students will flourish in. Essential components such as choice, time, access to books, and a supportive environment will lead to reading success, and yet how often do we take away any of these in order to serve our students better ("The Six Ts of Effective Elementary Literacy Instruction")? It therefore seems that our problem does not lie in what we know, but rather in what we do. In an effort to bolster student comprehension, we seem to have beaten the love of reading out of our instruction. It is not too late to reclaim it, but first we need to get to know the very students we teach.

On the second day of school, we start our reading identity discovery when I ask my students to take the two-page survey on who they are as readers. While I have done it electronically, I have returned to the paper copy year after year because I want to keep their survey as they progress throughout the year. Keeping notes on 130+ students is not easy, nor is trying to figure out what is essential knowledge and what is not, but this initial reader survey gives me a much-needed starting point. They get unlimited time to fill it out, and I tell them that the answers are for my eyes only. Most are honest, and some have answers so raw that it almost seems as if they are daring me to change their minds. That night, as I sift through their truths to put them into their quarter 1 reading sheet (see appendix for sheet), I see the year before me; I see the identities that students have brought with them. I see the challenge ahead. Out of 126 students, 30% of them tell me that they did not read a single book this summer. Fifteen percent tell me they own less than ten books. Eighteen percent tell me that they only read when they have to. Twenty-seven percent tell me they hate reading. I am thankful for their answers, because now I know what I am up against. Now I know what reading habits we have to work with, and my mind starts to spin with ideas of the year to come.

Those initial thoughts in reading are so important. In fact, this is where our reading year starts—with students coming to terms with the biases and sometimes even baggage that they have with reading. While I wholeheartedly believe that we must be the loudest cheerleaders for reading, we cannot dismiss the truths that the students carry in our effort to change their minds.

Nowhere is this clearer to me than in the following exchange after a student had told me that she hated reading. As I was about to tell her that she had simply not found the right book, she stopped me mid-sentence to say, "And please don't tell me that I haven't found the right book yet because that's what all the teachers have said." So I instead swallowed my words and told her that we would try to find a better path for her, that I would support her every step of the way. So while I will continue to tell all children that profess to not be readers that they just have not found the right book yet, I will also listen to why they say so. In fact, this has been one of the biggest lessons my students have taught me throughout the years; that we teachers must embrace the emotions that come attached to their reading lives in order to strengthen their relationship.

The components we put the most emphasis on in our learning communities is what will shape our students' reading experiences for years to come. So if our focus is on compliance, teacher-led, and by the book, then that is what will dominate our students' reading experiences when they think of reading. We can continue to teach in a way that we hope will lead to more invested readers, or we can start to tweak the foundational components that we all work within to create opportunities for students to have high-quality reading experiences that are centered on discovering and strengthening who they are as individual readers.

Ask the Hard Questions

I try to help my students be passionate readers. To be the type of reader that sneaks reading in whenever they can, that bring books with them wherever they go, to be the kind of reader that cannot wait to read the next book they have on their list. I try to be a role model for this, but to do this I have realized that we must discuss why reading sucks.

I ask my students their thoughts on reading as part of one of our very first mini lessons. While many of them share such wonderful things about their love of reading, there is usually one brave enough who finally just says that reading is just not his thing. One year was no different when a child told me that "Reading sucks" and then waited for my reaction. I am not sure what the child expected, but instead of dismissing their notion as crazy, I created a poster asking them to list why reading sucks. As hand upon hand was raised, eager to share their truths, one child blurted out, "I don't think a teacher has ever asked me that."

He was right, of course. Never in my career as a teacher of reading had I stopped to ask children why reading was not the greatest thing in the world.

That day, though, since it presented itself, I figured it had to be dealt with head on. The kids were cautious at first, perhaps they felt I was trying to trick them, but soon they clamored to share their reasons so that they too could join the conversation.

Those are valid reasons why reading may not be the best thing for a child. Some children hate sitting still, others find it boring and time consuming, some hate that they are forced to read certain books or at a certain time, perhaps they feel pressured, perhaps they feel they are bad readers. What it all adds up to is a miserable reading experience. And that is what we have to fight.

In the end, I thanked the kids for their honesty, then asked them for their solutions, and at first they didn't quite have any. Then one child raised a hand and said, "Can we pick our own books?" "Yes." "Do we have to read a certain amount of minutes and log it?" "No, I said, I expect you to read every night and talk about your books." "Do we have to finish every book we start?" "No." With each question and answer, relief seemed to spread throughout the room. Perhaps reading would not suck as much as it had in the past, perhaps they would not hate it this year. Perhaps . . . and that is all I need. The seed that reading may not suck after all.

If we don't ask the question and face this reading demon, then we can't have the conversations that we need to have with these specific kids. Yes, most students will tell us that reading is amazing, whether they believe it or not. I hail the kids that have the strength to tell me how they really feel. How else will I ever change their minds?

Uncovering Student Reading Identities: Ideas for Change

I think an important thing is to have students set goals for themselves, as well as the teacher. Then you don't ask too much of them and can base the lessons on what you think they could work on or what they already know.

—Amber, seventh grader

When I was first asked to consider writing more about the reading experience we have created in our seventh grade learning community, I was not sure where to start. After all, it is hard to explain the big picture when it is supported by so many little changes that have been integrated throughout the years. Upon reflection, though, I realized that the strength of what we do in room 235D is in all of those small components of change. They arose from particular needs that my students expressed, they arose from obstacles we faced, and they arose from my desire to be a better teacher.

That is why this book is not a step-by-step program, but rather is meant as a reflection tool and idea generator as you continue in your own journey as a teacher of reading. This book, while infused with my own ideas, is therefore also built on the knowledge of many who also teach reading or research how to create better reading experiences. There is not one person I can point to as the most influential in my own professional growth, but instead I have a list of many whose advice, research, and ideas I continue to turn to as these changes develop further. I therefore encourage you to read research on best practices within reading, to read cornerstone texts about creating incredible reading environments, to follow the work of other teachers who are on their path of learning like you are, to reach out and share your own ideas, and finally, to ask the students you teach. Ask them how you can be a better teacher for all of them. Ask them what stops their love of reading. Ask them what type of experience they would like to have. There are many small changes we can implement within our reading learning communities, and so the following sections are not the only components we can change, but the ones that in my experience have made the biggest impact for us. Each component will have ideas for you to try, as well as reflection questions to push your thinking.

Component of Change: The Initial Reading Conference

Every child is smart in some way and teachers need to embrace that.

—Sam, seventh grader

While I encourage you to begin your students' reading exploration with a survey, having students take a survey is not enough. After all, they already know the answers they put down, and usually there has been no revelation for them. A survey will never change their mind about who they are as readers; instead, it is truly just meant as a way for us to catch up with who they are. We must therefore use the information we gather with them and fast. One way to do is this is to follow up with individual conferences to ask them what they see as most important in their answers, not revealing what stuck out to you. This initial meeting will also serve as a foundation for the check-ins you will do throughout the year. It is important that we let the students speak more than we do, as we need for them to realize that their reading identity is not one determined by us, but one that they solely carry responsibility for. Too often our nonreaders, whether they be developing, resistant, or simply too busy, are waiting for the teacher to tell them who they are as readers and what they should read. Many of our readers would like us to take charge from the very first conference; after all, it is much easier to resist the urge to read when it is tied to another person's interest. So that first conference sets the tone—it is their classroom, it is their journey, and we are their guide, not the final authority. This is also why that first conference needs to be one that they see themselves as in control of. The point of the conference is therefore not just for us to take more notes, but instead to truly listen and support as students formulate their own questions and also direct their own path. While we should take notes as needed, do not have all of your questions planned out, but instead allow yourself to be guided by the direction the student wants to take. By doing this, students start to become more accustomed to self-reflection and realizing the control they have over the reading journey they are on.

Questions you could ask at those initial conferences include, but are not limited to:

◆ Who are you as a reader?
◆ Why do you say this?
◆ Tell me more about that.
◆ Where do you see yourself in a month as a reader?
◆ What are good habits that you have?
◆ What are bad habits that you have?
◆ What are the most important things I should know about you as a reader?

In our initial conference, students typically set up a reading goal, both quantity and specific accomplishments, that will guide them until our next conference or whenever they are asked to reflect next, whichever comes first. Self-reflection becomes a tool we use quite often throughout the year because students need to see how they are growing. It is not enough for me to marvel at the fact that they are changing, they need to realize it themselves. So every once in a while, have the students write down a few reading goals and have them reflect on the ones they have been working on. I used to have their reading goals tied in with skills; for example, a child set a goal of wanting to analyze text better or look for more signposts from *Notice & Note*, but I realized that he or she did not care about those goals. They were set and then forgotten because they carried no personal meaning to the child. So the goals have now shifted. Now, they focus on perhaps finishing a series, on sharing a book experience with a friend, on changing one's reading habits. Later on when I move to regular reading check-ins, I will ask about their reading goals and their answers will shape our conversation. This allows me to pursue a direction that is meaningful to them. The goals do not become our be all and end all, but instead one more step in our path of becoming more invested readers. Also, the goal setting itself is a clue as to where there are in their reading journey; not only are we looking for whether they reach a goal, but do they even know how to set an attainable one? Encouraging students to really think about what they need to move forward as readers is therefore paramount in their reading identity formation. If they cannot formulate a goal, then they do not know themselves as readers and thus cannot become connected to themselves as passionate readers.

Questions you can ask to help a child set a goal include, but are not limited to:

- What are reading habits you would like to change?
- How much time do you spend on reading right now outside of class?
- How do you pick a book?
- Who do you discuss books with?
- What type of reader would you like to become?
- What type of reader are you?
- What speed do you read at and how do you know?
- What does that speed mean to you?

Starting our year with exploring who students are as readers is paramount to any of the future work we will do. We cannot create a personal approach to each child if we do not know who the child is. However, we often feel that with increased numbers of students, it is this personal connection that is sacrificed. I know that it takes me a lot longer to get to know my students than it ever did when I was their only content teacher. Yet, creating these opportunities within our curriculum to truly get to know the students that we are teaching allows us, in turn, to create opportunities for them to explore who they are. This starts with us asking questions and then it continues with conversation. So do not dismiss even the small moments of conversation you can build in with your learners throughout the year. Start early, and do it as often as you can, this is where the foundation is laid.

Questions to ponder as you plan for your initial reading experiences:

- How would you like your learners to feel after your first few days together?
- What are important things to know about your learners that can shape your time together?

◆ Where in your time together can you build in more time to have conversation?

◆ How can your learners take ownership over the reading journey they are about to embark on?

◆ How will you handle the information that is provided to you?

◆ How will what you uncover shape the time you have together?

Focusing on the Individual

Whatever the program is you have to implement in your reading curriculum, there is a way to create a focus on the children and their individual reading journey. What matters is how we focus our journey using specific questions and taking the time for the students to explore their own identities. So what are some tried and true ideas that you could implement starting today, beyond investing in great books, offering choice, and giving them time?

Diversity in books. The #WeNeedDiverseBooks movement has really gained momentum the past few years, and rightfully so. Our students need to be able to find themselves and their lives within the books we have. Not just across racial lines or economic lines, but also in the narratives of their identity. So reflect critically on the book choices you have. Is your library offering a chance for students to explore their own identity and be exposed to others as well? What are the characterizations present of certain religions or racial groups? We need books that reflect the society we live in as whole, not just the one that we teach in. Another great hashtag to follow is #OwnVoices that highlights diverse books written by authors whose background mirrors that of their characters.

Leaving time to talk books. Too often, we overschedule our lessons and don't leave time to just talk about what we are reading and why it is amazing. So find holes in your schedule where students can just talk books without any project attached to it. Can they turn and talk when they would like to? Are students book-talking books or somehow sharing their reading lives? Is there a space for them to display the books they love that is not dominated by you? Is there always a project attached to finishing a book or can students simply start a new book?

Student recommendations. We talk about books quite a bit, both in structured and unstructured ways. We do 1-minute speed book dating, where students face each other in two long rows and one side recommends the book in a minute. Once the timer buzzes, they go to the next person and recommend it. We also have informal share in both their groups, as well as in front of the class. How can your students start to recommend more books to each other?

Can you use social media for them to share their thoughts? Do they have space in the curriculum to share? Instagram is a more recent addition in our learning community for this purpose. Many of my students are on Instagram and use it on a daily basis, but I had not seen a need for it in my own personal life. At least not until I realized how I could use a picture and a hashtag to share book recommendations. While I used to maintain a reading review blog, I often viewed updating it as a task rather than an enjoyable experience, and so I just didn't, leaving me with no outlet to share my reading. Insert Instagram here. Now with a quick picture of a book cover and a hashtag (#pernillerecommends), I can quickly share a book recommendation with my own followers and anyone else using the same hashtags. People can leave comments or ask questions and it is easy to maintain. This year we have taken it a step further by creating a school-wide hashtag (#OMSreads) and asking students to post their own book recommendations on it. While mostly I am the one who posts to it, several of my students have commented that they follow me on it. By using the tools students are already using, we are creating a school-wide awareness of the reading lives we all have and a place where anyone can get a good recommendation. For those students without Instagram or a device, I post the pictures for them, taken during our 10 minutes of independent reading time.

It is judgment free. I am not the reading police, and while I continually recommend books to students, I will not stop them from reading a book, nor will I judge them based on what they are reading. Sometimes your strongest readers need a break; other times your developing readers need a challenge. Letting them figure out what they need at a particular time is incredibly empowering for students and definitely necessary. So when a child starts to read a book and shows it to you, does your facial expression give you away? Do you have an open mind when it comes to how students select the books they want to read or abandon?

Celebrating the reread. I reread picture books all of the time and often find myself gravitating toward certain books. *The Poisonwood Bible* is a book I have read several times, relishing the vague recollection of what happens but also discovering the text in new way each time. Too often, we assume that students are rereading because they lack inspiration, but that may not be the case. Some kids are rereading to discover more about the text—that is true close reading. When a child chooses to reread a book, what is your reaction? Do you ask why? Do you know which books are being reread in your learning community?

No need for speed. Because we are reading log free, we have no need to track minutes or pages. Students read as much as they can in our independent reading time, and I only ask them to write down the title. We do a 25 book challenge for all students, or higher if need be, and all students keep track of how many books they have read. Larger books count for more than one, so that students are not discouraged from reading thick books, but can read whatever they want. And yes, audiobooks or graphic novels count as well.

Creating reading role models. Students need reading role models, and not just adult ones. I love being a passionate reader, and it is something I highlight any chance I get in our learning community, but more importantly, students need to see students who are reading role models as well. We need to create communities of readers where students have room to discover each other as individuals so they can learn from each other. So offer up room for conversations so that students may find each other. Also search beyond the classroom. We use Twitter to connect with other readers and the authors whose books we love. My students use this tool, often through my personal account although we also have a class account, to reach out to authors whose books they love. When George finished *Booked* by Kwame Alexander, he quickly asked me to tweet him this, "George would like to know, will you write a sequel and what is in the box?" A few minutes later, Kwame Alexander wrote back, "Tell George that both of those are very good questions." From that moment on, George told everyone that would listen that he and Kwame were best friends. That connection to an author and the work of that author cannot be underestimated. We need more of those in our learning communities, especially for the students who despise reading or who have never found a book they really love. Yet Twitter does not just connect us with the authors we love, it also connects us with other learning communities. Often we will send out questions for others to answer, or answer questions created by other learning communities. We will reach out to experts or link to our work in the learning community. Twitter allows us a portal to the world, all in the time it takes to type up to 140 characters.

Let them order books. If a children say they cannot find a book they love, then I pull out a Scholastic catalog or get on Amazon and I let them choose a book. I use bonus points when I can or I buy the book myself if I need to. Sometimes simply being able to completely choose a brand new book means that a child will at least try to read the books.

Crack your hardest nut. You know those kids who really hate reading and almost flaunt it every chance they get. Spend your energy on them, because often they are influencing the way their peers are thinking. So they are the ones I continually pass books to, they are the ones I am always talking books with, and they are the ones that I try to get be a reading role model if I can get them hooked.

Embrace mature books. I have taught children whose parents have never owned a home, or who own several, or who have lived solely on the generosity of strangers. I have taught children who have watched their parents get arrested. Children who have watched family members drink until they passed out, shoot up, or take pills. I have taught children whose earliest memories were of a parent walking out on them. Children who have found God, or Allah, or nothing at all. I have taught children who believe that family matters above everything else and some who do not know what family means. I have taught children who from an early age knew they were not straight or the gender they were born with. Every year I teach a new child whose story breaks my heart and makes me question humanity. We probably all have, whether we know it or not. We wear so many hats as teachers, as parents. Sometimes we wear many at once, our roles always fluid, striving to do the very best we can for every child that is in our care. We carry so many words that our students entrust us with. Snippets of their life stories as they try to realize who they want to be while they grow up in our learning communities. As they try to accept themselves and the persons they see themselves becoming. So make sure our libraries offer choices that students will actually want to read. Make sure our libraries have books that will reflect the lives our students live and also create an opportunity for them to see what other children may go through. So embrace the tough books, the ones that may make you a little bit uncomfortable, the ones you know will be read when you place them in your library. Because we do not always know what our students are going through, sometimes no one does, so the least we can do is make sure there are books for them in our schools that will guide them.

Component of Change: Supporting Honest to Goodness Choice in Reading

Have a classroom library and give choice to what books kids read. We are more willing to read if we get to choose what it is, rather than being forced to read a certain book.
—Kaitlyn, seventh grader

If you looked at the reading life of my daughter, Theadora, a sparkly 8-year-old, you might assume that she does not know who she is as a reader. One day she carries her picture books, leaving piles around the house as she flips through pages, eager to look at the next one, and the next she asks me to keep driving so we can listen more to Harry Potter. She jumps from genre to genre, nonfiction to fiction, and leaves a wake of books behind her. To some she may look lost or at the very least like a reader in need of rescue, yet dig a little deeper, and you will see that she is not a reader in crisis, but instead a reader who is firmly entrenched in her own reading choices. She does not care what others think she needs to read, she reads what she wants and navigates it as best as she can. In fact, one day she declared to me, "Mom, I have decided I am an awesome reader because I like to read books!" This coming from a child who has been in reading intervention with incredible teachers since she started school. Access and choice of books has made the biggest difference to this developing reader and will do the same for all of our students. For them, this is what we should fight for—an opportunity to explore who they are as readers without being confined to a level, a Lexile, a zone, or a point score.

In the spring of 2016, I polled more than 1,200 students in North America ranging from the age of 8 to 13. While the poll was mostly focused on how they felt about book abandonment, I asked a question I always ask in our learning community as well—what do you wish all teachers of reading would let you do? This simple question has shaped my own reading instruction for years, and I was not disappointed, or surprised, at the overwhelming answer; give us choice! Let us pick the books we want to read, how we read them, and also how we interact with them. This pillar of what it means to be a reader is one that our students are begging to have, and I was not surprised that choice was the most requested component of a better reading experience, because choice happens to be the very first thing we seem to take away from students as they learn to read.

While a reading expert such as Regie Routman is correct when she states, "If the book is too difficult, it will lead to frustration; too little of a challenge will lead to boredom," we must not forget the desires of our students to self-select the book they want to read based on want and not just need. It appears that in our eagerness to make sure students are reading "just right" books or "good fit" texts, books that fit the criteria set forth by experts, we have diminished the voice of the very reader who will read them—that of the student. Instead, as students start to develop their reading habits, we tell them to stick to their level so that they will always be appropriately challenged. But we forget to wonder, what if a child wants to struggle? What if he or she wants to try for a harder text? As one child answered on the book abandonment survey I gave, "I wish we didn't have to read in our zone because we need to develop our reading abilities and some really good books aren't in my zone which is bad because I like to read books that mean something." Books that mean something; sometimes these are left behind as we chase after the elusive "just right" books. However, this notion of student choice is not meant as a dismissal of the research on the right fit book. As Richard Allington says, "Whenever we design an intervention for struggling readers, the single-most critical factor that will determine the success of the effort is matching struggling readers with texts they can actually read with a high level of accuracy, fluency, and comprehension" (2009). And I would say that goes for any child; we must create conditions where they will be able to find books that will offer them not only successful reading experiences, but also engaging ones. As Regie Routman wrote, "A carefully designed program that includes teaching how to choose a book, monitoring the process, and evaluating can impact reading achievement" (Routman 2003). And so those exact conditions are what I try to create year after year with my many students, all within the short time frame of the 45-minute English language arts learning community.

Yet it is not just the words of experts that guide me, it is from the experiences with children through the years that I have become an ardent defender of the right to choose a book. That does not mean that systems like the five-finger rule (where you put a finger up or down every time you come across a word that you do not understand; if you reach five, then the book is too hard for you and should not be chosen), or the "Goldilocks rule" (Too easy, just right, too hard) as coined by Regie Routman, or even the levels created by Fountas and Pinnell (books are given a readability level in the form of a letter to help guide student book selections) should be dismissed. There is immense value in teaching children these easy-to-remember short cuts or scaffolds for how to best select a book, but that is exactly it—they are scaffolds, and scaffolds need to be removed at some point. So while levels, or fingers, or books that fit just right are all wonderful ways for students to start to think about what they want or need to read, it cannot chase them all the way through their teen years. We must create opportunities within our instruction where students learn to rely on their own systems for selecting a text and will also know when to abandon a text. We must keep our eye on the end goal—to help students become self-sufficient readers that can walk into any book environment and successfully select a book that will matter to them. As one child told me when asked why students dislike reading, "I dislike reading when teachers pick the book, that's why." We were never supposed to take over a child's reading journey; we were never supposed to be the only authority on what a child should read. We are meant to guide, to cheer on, to push, to challenge, and to always encourage. To be reading role models that believe that all children have the capability to choose a great book that works for them when they have been taught how to. My goal, therefore, is always for students to have this response when asked why they like reading, "I like reading because it brings a moment of silence to the world." May we all be able to create communities filled with moments of silence.

The Experience of Real Choice Without Levels, Lexiles, or Points

I think my reading teacher is so great; she lets me choose my books!
—Anonymous seventh grader

One might think that creating an environment filled with student book choice is easy and yes, for many of our students, not much guidance is needed. Many of our students come to us in the later years of schooling with an inherent sense of who they are as readers, the types of books they like to read, where they like to read them, and also which book they will be reading next. We can be grateful for the prior reading experiences that these children have had both in the learning communities they have been a part of, but also in their homes. While these children need new genres to try out, opportunities to challenge themselves, and as much time as possible to continue reading, our job with our well-established readers are not just as cheerleader, but also as a protector of their already well-established reading identities. These kids deserve to have meaningful reading experiences just as our non-established readers do. However, for some of our kids, the notion of choice does not induce jubilation but just becomes one more thing to do. One more thing they now have to worry about or force their way through. I think of one of my students who was not in the least delighted when told he could choose whatever he wanted to read and instead asked if he then could choose to not read. He seemed dismayed when I told him that not reading was simply not a choice. So how do we establish communities founded on choice when students do not want to take the time to select a great book?

We start with our library collections, which is why an entire chapter is dedicated to the classroom library in this book, as well as great books themselves (to see some of the favorite books in room 235D, go to https://pernillesripp.com/our-favorite-books/). Simply put, for students to select a great book, we must have great books. A repeated word of caution, though, our classroom libraries should not just be catered around our taste but truly reflect the many interests of our students. This is why you will find me shopping the sports section at Half Price Books about once a month, not because I cheer for any team, but because I know that the sports biographies of famous football and basketball players will get snatched up on Monday by some of my less-than-avid readers. So will hunting guides, mermaid books, and anything that has to do with sports—all books I tend to not read. It also bears repeating that while large quantity libraries are to be desired and striven for, no library starts out large. Instead, focus on the few but great books that you know will entice readers to become invested and pay attention to your changing population. A few years ago, I could not keep dystopian young adult fiction on the shelves, and while it remains popular, there is now a push for more free verse novels. I have therefore purposefully invested more in free verse books lately because my more resistant readers, those who really fight me in class, gravitate toward this deep but more easily digestible sort of writing. So tune into what your students are gravitating toward. This is why I love crafting our book shopping days and then participating in them, because I get to experience what students are pulled toward and what they are not.

As your library collection grows, you must model what it means to choose freely. Do not give "pretend choice," where students can only choose from a preselected set of books. Often this practice stems from our helpfulness as we guide our students to only choose a book that seems to be at their right "level." In fact, when I was a fifth grade teacher, I was told to level my library, or at least a part of it. When I asked why, I was told that it needed to be done so that students could find their right fit books and it had been suggested by the curriculum program we were adapting. Yet, in our reading community, this was already happening; my students knew how to select a book, and the few who didn't were learning ways to do it beyond that of a level. Being a fifth grade teacher meant that most students had many different ways of determining whether a book would be the right fit for them or not, which was something we had developed throughout the year. Just like when they went to our school library, the students knew to pick up books, flip through the pages, and determine whether they wanted to read a book by reading a few pages and so on. They knew to ask a friend, to try a book on for size, or even to have me book shop with them. The last thing they needed was a level to restrict their choice.

I understand why leveling a library might seem like a great idea on paper; after all, we love when we can quickly point a child in the right direction. We love when many children can book shop at the same time without our assistance, using only the scaffolds we have set in place. We love when we can hand a kid a stack of books without having read them and say, "these are for you because their level told me so." Whether Lexile, Fountas and Pinnell, AR score, or another contrived form of measurement, data that breaks down a reader seems to have permeated our educational experience. And it makes sense, after all, with our obsession with quantifiables and standardized testing. We love when we can break something complicated down to something tangible. But reading identity was never meant to be broken down like this, and neither was a child.

Levels are not meant to be a child's label, but a teacher's tool, to quote Irene Fountas (2013). They were never meant to be hindrances to children exploring books, nor were they meant to be the focal point of how we know a reader. They were meant for guiding us, the teachers, as we planned our instruction in order to help students succeed at the reading strategies we were teaching. And yet, I have seen entire classroom libraries, and even entire school ones, designated by letters. I have heard from librarians who were told that they had to police their book checkouts to make sure a child had picked the correct books. I have heard this from teachers who have seen children stop reading because they were only allowed to pick from certain boxes, and from parents who have despaired at the few books their children bring home. Levels have even shown up in our book order magazines to help parents guide their child's decision. I cannot be the only one that is horrified at what this is doing to our readers.

You see, levels, much as a child's reading level, is meant to be a scaffold. We start our early readers by guiding them using every tool that we have, including the reading level they are at, as we try to help them figure out how to pick books by themselves. Having a level or a letter helps them on their beginning journeys as readers. So does the five-finger rule. Yet at some point, our conversation needs to move beyond the letter, the point score, the Lexile, or whatever other designator we have. We need to shift the exploration of reader identity past the easy and into the hard. We need to start asking students what draws them to books and what keeps them there. How do they know when a book will be successful for them? How do they book shop? How do they keep track of what they want to read next? It has to be more than just because the level said it would work for them. Those conversations take time, they take energy, and they take us knowing our students in a deeper way than just their supposed reading ability. It also takes investment from our readers, which again, takes time within our curriculum. If our goal is to create reading experiences where students will leave our learning communities and school knowing who they are as readers, then our conversation has to extend beyond their level or score.

So before we level our entire library, or even tell a child what level they are at, remember that, depending on our students, it may be not only unnecessary, but also damaging to their future reading life. As educators, our main goal is to create independent learners, yet the very levels we use to help students reach independence means that they are not. Moving beyond a level, a label, or whatever else we have decided will break down a child for us, must be a priority as teachers of reading. We must ensure that their reading identity does not hinge on an outside indicator, but instead on their own understanding of themselves as readers. That takes time, and while time seems to be something we have very little of in school, it is an investment into their future life as adult readers. In the "Kid and Family Reading Report" produced by Scholastic every year, 51% of kids reported that the reason they picked a book that was above their level was because it was something that was of interest to them. ("Kid and Family Reading Report" 2014). Is that not how we select books as adults as well?

Levels were never meant to confine children's reading life or choices, they were meant to help them on their way. Much as we remove training wheels from a bike when a child is old enough, we must remove the levels as well. We owe it to the future adults we teach. So instead of succumbing to the easiness of levels, open up your entire library for all students, including audiobooks and picture books. In my experience, students will grab books that fall within their own designated comfort zone most of the time. However, it is okay for a child to decide to work through a complex text—this is also part of their reading growth. So while reading experts argue both for and against leveled text, I think in our learning community we need both texts that will fit our readers and their desires, as well as those that will push them a little as readers. As Gay Ivey and Peter Johnston wrote, "Students should be expected to read widely from texts they want to read, building their background knowledge and vocabularies while developing morally, emotionally, and intellectually" (2013). So ask yourself—is the reading experience you are creating allowing children the opportunity to read widely? And if not, why not?

Questions to ponder as you reflect on how reading levels or scores are used in your learning community:

◆ Is the data collected valid for each child?
◆ What is the data actually used for?
◆ When the data does not seem accurate, what is done with it?
◆ What are the advantages to knowing the reading level of a child?
◆ What are the disadvantages to knowing the reading level of a child?
◆ What information would be useful for learners to receive about themselves as readers?
◆ Is learner input used to shape instruction?
◆ How do artificial measurements of reading success influence the decisions made in your learning community or school?
◆ Are reading levels, Lexiles, or point systems such as Accelerated Reader helping or hurting *all* of your learners?

Component of Change: Book Shopping As a Way to Grow Community

By not forcing kids to read certain books teachers can help kids love reading more. These days, most won't care if it's a classic book. Kids want to read what kids want to read.

—Joel, seventh grader

All teachers know that even when we are on break we are thinking of the days to come with our learners; my life is no different. All throughout summer, I gather up as many new enticing reads as I can, lugging them into school excited to see the piles gather and grow. Whether it is from the generosity of publishers who hand out advanced review copies at conferences like NerdCamp or ILA, or from my frequent visits to Half Price Books, Books4School, or independent bookstores that I frequent on my travels, I always have stacks of books waiting on the first day of school that mostly have never been read before. On one of our first days of school, as students enter the learning community, they are greeted by piles of books placed on each pod or cluster of tables. Some kids are instantly drawn to the piles, while others look at them with disdain. I always enjoy observing the varied responses to the prospect of having to pick up an actual book. Before we start to explore the books, we set up one of our biggest tools of the year—the to-be-read list inspired by the ideas shared by both Donalyn Miller and Susan Kelley in *Reading in the Wild* and Penny Kittle in *Book Love*. This simple tool is one of our biggest difference makers when it comes to steering children on a path toward reading. This is also a tool that may cause a reaction in some of our most ardent nonreaders, an outright refusal to use it; however, I am steadfast in this approach. Every reader needs to know what he or she will read next, and every reader needs a way to keep track of it. Together we flip to the first page of what will become our reader's notebook for the year, and we create four columns: Rating, Title, Author, and Genre. That is all we need right now, or at least that is all I ask my students to create. We add a tab divider to the bottom of the page for easy finding, and then I ask them to come on over, our signal for story time. As they gather in front of me, I pull out a favorite picture book, *How to Read a Story* by Kate Messner, and after reading the book aloud, I ask, "How do you find books to read next?" Together we create a chart with what we do; we read the back, we read a few pages, we ask for recommendations, we follow favorite authors, genres, or series and so on. Inevitably we run out of things to say, and sometimes a large way is omitted on purpose—judging a book by its cover. In fact, one year with my seventh graders I had to prompt them by asking, "What is the one thing you wish you could say but have not?" to which several children immediately responded, "I look at the cover!" And of course they do, we all do, that is why editors and publishing houses spend so much money and time on choosing the seemingly perfect cover. So we discuss how judging a book by its cover is perfectly acceptable, as long as that is not the only thing we judge it by. In fact, I always have a book or two handy with covers that are not-so-great, in my opinion, but that anyway are stories I love. I sneak these two books in as book talks and then place them in the piles as well. We also discuss the need for abandoning books, something that will be discussed more in detail, but it is always a point I make early on in the year. I speak of my own book abandonment habits and how part of knowing yourself as a reader is knowing when a book is not the right match for you at the time. That also means that we need to know what is a good fit for us, which directly plays into our book shopping habits, as well as our to-be-read list. Finally, we develop a few guidelines for book shopping. They are usually along these lines, but vary slightly from year to year:

◆ You must book shop with your to-be-read list and a pencil in hand.
◆ You must try to find at least five titles to add to your list, but more is preferred. If you can't, speak to a friend or Mrs. Ripp.
◆ You should talk to others while book shopping and show off interesting books to others.
◆ You should look at covers, read the back, and perhaps even read a few lines before you decide.
◆ Book shopping can take as long as it needs to, and it can happen when needed in class as well.
◆ Ask for help if you cannot find any books that seem interesting; I will then offer to walk with you.
◆ Books may not be checked out until all English classes have book shopped, then they are first come, first served.

And then they are off, most eagerly browsing, eagerly touching the books just as I had hoped. Scribbling, exploring, and deciding on possible titles to explore all in the span of the next 15 to 20 minutes. These are our established readers, the kids that will help us widen our reading community. Most kids are engaged, most kids are happily browsing or at least going through the motions, but perhaps your class will be like mine; you will have those few kids where book shopping is about the last thing they would like to do, where you have to give repeated reminders to even get them to touch a book. So then what? I have found that a non-pushy discussion with them is always best. If children refuse to book shop, I always wonder what has led them to this point? How many terrible experiences have they had with reading to not even want to browse books? What else is happening in their heads right now where this seemingly relaxed reading and community builder is such a hard thing? I ask questions, as many as I comfortably can, and I focus on the child in front of me. I do not force them to book shop, as that will only push them further away, but instead try to bring a few books to them. If they also refuse them, then I let them take a break from me for a little while. I check in with them again and see how they are doing now, but in the end, if they didn't book shop that day, that is ok. I will keep trying, I will keep asking, and I will keep trying to understand why they are at this point in their reading lives. I deem it a success every year when by the end of class that day, most students are excited to try some of the new titles, even if a few are not.

After this initial experience, book shopping becomes a pillar of our community as readers; it is something we spend as much time on as we need and something that I spend more time on now than I ever did before. This decision matters. As Sam wrote when I asked him about his reading experience in our classroom, "Reading has been great for me this year because of the book shopping we do." Something as simple as browsing books, something that we often assume that students, our learners, know how to do well, is something we must embrace with all our kids. If we don't already. If you need proof, ask your learners what makes for a great reading experience. I will hazard a guess that most of them will tell you that they need to find a great book but that they struggle with this. Without fail, year after year, students share that they like reading only when they have the right book, that they cannot find the right book, that they have never read a book they truly like. And so the more I teach, the more I realize that book shopping and how to find a great book is one of the biggest skills we can teach students before they leave us. And the more I teach, the more I realize that there were more effective ways to do it well than what I had previously done. Once again, the inspiration to tweak the process comes from the ideas shared by my students. Feel free to use these ideas as a way to evaluate your own process and then proceed from here. Remember to always ask your students how this process can be more valuable to them and then adapt accordingly.

Old way: Books are displayed like a bookstore, in a row on the bookshelves.
New way: Books are grouped together in bins by genre, topic, or author.

What difference does it make? The bins can be placed on tables as a group and students can easily flip through them. Students can also more easily identify where books are that may capture their interest. It also means that book covers are displayed out, catching the eye of readers as they sit in the learning community.

Old way: Books are randomly placed back in their genre bins.
New way: I place all books back in the library taking care with which book is at the front of the bin, thus facing out to the class.

What difference does it make? Much like bookstores and libraries change their displays, so must we, so the fronts of our bins become mini displays that are ever changing. This is also a great way for "older" books to be discovered. Students see amazing books waiting to be read whenever they are in our learning community.

Old way: A designated book shopping time.
New way: Book shopping whenever they need it.

What difference does it make? Kids need a new book whenever they need a new book. They should not have to wait until a designated time or day to book shop. Encouraging them to book shop, whenever it is needed, means that they always a have a new book to read. This also means that I can see how students book shop on their own and what their habits are, which, in turn, helps me help them become better book shoppers. As one child told me on the last day of school, "You know what made the biggest difference to me? The books were always right there."

Old way: Book shopping was mostly silent as students tried to get through it as quickly as possible.
New way: Book shopping is a social event at least every few weeks.

What difference does it make? One of the things we work a lot on is creating a community of readers, and that community comes from finding your reading peers. So when students can book shop and are encouraged to discuss books as they go, we are creating ties that bind us together as readers. I jump in and out of conversations as they book shop, perhaps highlighting a few books or helping a child that seems to be lost, but I love the conversations that I overhear about books and why a certain one looks amazing. This also shows that I am not the center of book shopping, because students should not rely on me to be the one that finds them a great book, at least not at the end of the year, so the book shopping event plants the seed for them to rely on each other, rather than just the teacher.

Old way: Book shopping meant just new books.
New way: Book shopping piles are now a mix of new books and old favorites.

What difference does it make? While we all love brand new books, there are so many great books published in earlier years. I put these in the piles with the brand new shiny books so that students can be introduced to them as well. I love when a child sees a loved book and has to share it with others to recommend it.

Old way: Book shopping lasts a few minutes.
New way: Book shopping takes the time it takes.

What difference does it make? Book shopping should take time; after all, students should be flipping through pages, perhaps reading a few, looking at the covers, and discussing books with each other. I ask my students to slow down and savor the moment; this helps them understand that book shopping is not just something we get through, it is something we enjoy.

Old way: Teacher as the first stop for book recommendations.
New way: To-be-read list as the first stop.

What difference does it make? Their to-be read list is my way of helping them rely on themselves rather than just on the teacher. So while I love book shopping and recommending books, I also need to teach students that they can rely on themselves. So when children ask me for a great new book to read, I ask them to find their to-be-read list first. This year our list is in our reader's notebooks, which stay in the learning community so the students always have access to it.

Old way: Book talks once in a while.
New way: Book talks every day.

What difference does it make? Inspired by Penny Kittle and her book *Booklove*, I book talk a book every day. These can be books I have read or books that are brand new to us. I try to book talk a new book every class, because kids want to check out the books right away so it is not fair to tell them to wait until the end of the day. If the book has a book trailer, I show that as well, as the impact of visual media when it comes to "selling" a book cannot be underestimated. My bigger goal, though, is that students take over these book talks and they start to recommend books to each other. Again, trying to shift the responsibility back on themselves rather than the teacher to find them books.

Old way: Book shopping guidelines apply just within the learning community.
New way: Book shopping guidelines apply to the library as well.

What difference does it make? I have noticed that students who know how to book shop in our learning communities sometimes flounder in the larger school library. Help them make the connection between the habits they establish with you when they are about to go to the library. Also browse with them, otherwise, for some kids, going to the library will just be one more time they will be trying to avoid books at all costs.

A final idea for better book shopping is also to have a stack of books ready for the kid that just hates reading. These should be some of the books that have had the most success with other kids that really have written off reading. I pay attention to what the game changer books are for my seventh graders and will often pull these out when I help children who say they hate reading find a book. It is amazing what some of these suggestions have done for planting a seed about how reading is maybe not the worst thing in the whole world. Some of our most recent game changer books are *Reality Boy* by A.S. King, *Monster* by Walter Dean Myers, *The Crossover* by Kwame Alexander, *All American Boys* by Brendan Kiely and Jason Reynolds, *The Absolutely True Diary of a Part Time Indian* by Alexis Sherman, *Rhyme Schemer* by K.A. Holt, and *Orbiting Jupiter* by Gary D. Schmidt. All of these books seem to catch my most ardent self-proclaimed nonreaders at some point in the year; I am so grateful to the authors.

Questions to ponder as you think of your established book shopping guidelines:

◆ What small change would bring more readers to your library?
◆ How are books placed back into your library?
◆ When can students book shop in their day with you?
◆ How can book shopping become an event rather than a to-do?
◆ Which must-read favorites have no students discovered yet?
◆ How do the students connect with each other and you while they book shop?
◆ How can students create and maintain an easily accessible to-be-read list?
◆ Is book shopping an event in your learning community?
◆ How often do you or students book talk a book?
◆ How can you partner with your librarian to support the book selection process?

Component of Change: Embracing Audiobooks for All

Teachers should let students listen to audiobooks because they might find their favorite book like I did.

—Ariel, seventh grader

Another component of our choice-based learning community is the right to listen to audiobooks and have them count toward a student's personal reading goal. While this is a newer component of our learning community's foundational rights, it is one I have embraced wholeheartedly due to the successful experiences it has provided some of my most resistant readers. In fact, several students the last few years have had incredible reading experiences. These kids who have never liked reading are begging for the next book, begging for more time to listen. Providing them access to audiobooks means that they can comprehend the words without having to struggle through the decoding. Accessing stories that they have heard their friends talk about. No longer looking at the easier books while they long for something with more substance. Those children are becoming readers with the help of audiobooks. As one child wrote, "Audiobooks are very helpful for when kids want to read a harder book than they usually can." Some may say that listening to an audiobook does not count as reading, I certainly used to balk at it counting toward any reading goal, yet my students have once again made me change my tune. Sure, there are cognitive differences in the processes that happens when we read with our eyes versus our ears; however, the skills that we are able to utilize through the listening to an audiobook are monumental in building further reader success and should not be considered "cheating" (Willingham 2016). So what has adding (and investing in audiobooks) done for our students?

Provided Equity in Reading Experience

Students who read significantly below their grade level are able to access the same texts as their peers. This matters when we create reading communities, because they no longer feel different when they book shop. Now, when they browse the books, they can select any book they are interested in and we can get it for them either through Overdrive or Audible.

Supported Critical Thinking Skills

Students can develop critical thinking skills without having to spend enormous brainpower on decoding. Decoding is still taught and supported through other texts; however, they now have a text that we can practice deeper thinking with that actually has deeper meaning. Not "just right" text that doesn't provide us with the complex relationships that make for such powerful stories.

Reignited a Passion for Reading

Often students who are developing readers start to hate reading. And I get it; when you are constantly in struggle mode, it can be so tiring, so having access via an audiobook lets students finally enjoy a story. They can be in the zone with the book because their brain is not occupied with the work of having to read, creating a deep immersion into the reading experience.

Provided New Strategies for Teaching Reading

I can now pull out segments of text to use with a student, knowing that he or she has the proper background knowledge, which is a key component when we build understanding. I do not have to reference the entire text, but instead can have them focus on the skill at hand. This therefore allows me to support their comprehension growth more efficiently.

Given Us a Gateway Into Reading With Their Eyes

Oftentimes, my developing readers harbor enormous hesitancy when it comes to veering out of their known texts. They are quick to dismiss, abandon, and feign disinterest, all in the interest of saving face and saving them from yet another reading disappointment. However, students finding success within the audiobook world are building their courage, their stamina, and their desire to pick up print texts.

I could list more reasons—being exposed to amazing fluency, students feeling like they have relevant thoughts when it comes to discussion, building overall reading self-esteem, planting high-interest books in the hands of students to see them become "the books to read," even changing the reading dynamics within a learning community.

In the end, I wonder whether it really matters whether having students listen to audiobooks is cognitively not exactly the same as when they read with their eyes. If our true goal of teaching reading is to make students fall in love with books, then audiobooks are a must for our learning communities. And so is the notion that they count as real reading. No longer should we denounce or diminish the very thing that can make the biggest difference to some of our students.

Ideas for incorporating audiobooks into your learning community:

Determine how students will listen. Do students have access to their own devices on which they can listen to audiobooks, or should a few be purchased for students to listen in class? We have successfully implemented audio-listening stations on a few iPads available to all learners and keep them in the room where they are needed.

Determine where books will be accessed through. We have Overdrive available to us through our public library, so students can check out audiobooks through their own accounts on the app. We have also purchased an audiobook account where I can select two new audiobooks every month. These are then saved in the app and read by students.

Determine how students will access the actual choices. I have one account that the students all use to log into our purchased audiobooks. They use a common login and password to access the book selections.

Determine the choices of books. I always add my favorite highly rated books to our account, and I also ask for student recommendations. Just as in our print copy library, we must not let our own tastes dictate what is accessible to students.

Determine whether a child is ready to try a print book. Some of my students listen to audiobooks for months; however, I do discuss with them whether they are ready to attempt a print book. This is not to dismiss the value of the audio experience, but instead to challenge them further. We speak about a well-balanced diet of books, and this is one of the components of that diet.

The support of free choice within our learning community, the development of how to select a great book, as well as having access to the right books is paramount as we create experiences where readers thrive. But that is not all. We need to start celebrating and utilizing some of the bad habits that students have as they enter our learning communities. One of the biggest is book abandonment, the stalwart companions of resistant readers everywhere.

Component of Change: Book Abandonment—A Cause for Celebration, Not Disapproval

I'm reading more because I found better books than last year and I can abandon books. I pick out books that are my own choice now and not the teacher's.

—Cecelia, seventh grader

I used to think that when children abandoned a book, they simply had not given it enough of a chance. That the act of abandonment was a badge of honor; look at how I am not reading! That they abandoned books because it was a way to not read, after all, you cannot read when you do not have a book. So I helped them by creating rules . . . You cannot abandon a book until you are 50 pages in. You can only abandon one book, then the next one you have to read. You must tell me when you abandon a book so I can give you permission to do so. The rules were meant to discourage it, to make abandoning a book a hassle, to inspire students to give the book a proper chance. Other rules were created as necessary, and the rules were tightened whenever I met a serial book abandoner. While I had hoped that my rules would inspire more students to fall in love with reading, quite the opposite happened. Indeed, it inspired some of my students to hide their habits from me, which in turn made me keep more track of their reading. I spent a long time merely checking up on their reading logs, parent signature required, to see if they really were sticking with a book. Swept up in the policy, it was easy to lose focus on what really mattered—kids actually liking reading, not just kids reading. Because there is a vast difference. Several years of this book abandonment philosophy meant that my learning community was rife with fake reading. In fact, I had one child fake read a book that he was not allowed to abandon for weeks because I was sure he would fall in love with it at some point. Instead, he perfected the art of turning the page at the right time so that I could see his progress. When he finally "finished" the book and we discussed it, it was painfully clear that he had not read very much of it.

All of that time wasted, all because I thought I was teaching students what it means to be a real reader. My seventh graders remind me of the control and skill it takes to be a fake reader. They boast of their skills of not reading, of how they know what to say to fool the teachers, of how they would rather pretend to read than actually read the "stupid" book assigned to them. I am at once amazed at their skills and saddened at their determination and I shudder at my own decisions that led children to these opinions and actions. When children choose to master fake reading at such a level, we should all feel sad. Consequently, in the beginning of the year, many students come to us with preconceived notions of what the rules of book abandonment are, no matter the reading environment they come from. This is why we start from scratch every year because while I know that my students come to me from caring reading environments, they sometimes forget what that means over the summer. Rather than constantly remind them of what it was like in their previous learning community, we start over together, creating the type of student-centered, literacy-based learning community that we all would like to be a part of, and one of the pillars of that is to embrace the habits of my ardent book abandoners.

This conundrum with book abandonment and what we use it for in our reading explorations therefore is something I take great interest in. Sticking with books we hate is not what most adult readers do, at least not the readers I know. Most adult readers abandon books, whether we feel guilty over it or not, because we realize that there are thousands of books that we could be reading instead. We abandon because we know what great reading experiences should feel like. Books are sometimes abandoned after one page, other times after 200; we shelve the book or pass it on, content with the knowledge that this was not the book we needed to read at that moment, and we march on in our hunt for the next great read. Those who tend to not abandon books do an incredible job selecting books that they actually want to finish, therefore feeling anchored in their reading identity, much like the students who carefully select their books in our learning communities. Knowing this, I realized a few years ago that as teachers of reading we have a duty to reclaim the art of book abandonment to show our students that no book deserves to be fake read.

The first thing we do in our learning community is to confront it head on, because as Teri Lesene writes in *Reading Ladders*, "Sometimes I think we forget that beginning with where students are is essential" (7). In the first week of school, when the dust has settled a little bit, the students and I dive into our classroom library—a collection of many books I have amassed throughout the years. Book selection is a natural place to start as we start to discuss the library; how to choose a book is where we start, and inevitably we end up at "What happens if I don't like the book?" I used to give a long answer of choosing a book responsibly, of knowing oneself as a reader, but now have whittled the answer down. When children ask what to do if they do not like a book, my short answer is, "Don't read it." Meaning don't waste your time on a book that you do not like. This is not to say that I do not want students to stretch themselves as readers, I do, and I believe that part of our job as teachers of literacy is to challenge and push our students' abilities to comprehend increasingly difficult text. But that first week of school I want students to understand that part of our year together is for them to discover who they are as readers, and a part of that discovery is to recognize when a book is not working for them. For many of my students, I need to get them to want to pick up a book without feeling like it is a binding contract. Therefore, telling children that even if they start a book they may still abandon it gives them power over who they are as readers, and it is that sense of power that will make them more curious as to what books may offer in general. I now know that book abandonment is a sign of a larger problem. That it is not something most students pride themselves on but instead becomes yet another sign that reading is seemingly not for them. Simply put, book abandonment becomes proof of their continued failures as readers. And the students seem to not know what to do about it. So if teaching seventh graders (and fourth and fifth graders) has taught me anything, it is that we have to face it head on.

We start on the second day of school. After we get through our quick must do—labeling their composition notebook, which they will use as their reader's notebook—I share a few stories with them. All of the stories have one thing in common; they speak of previous reading mistakes that I have made as a teacher. I share the story of how I used to read *Tales of a Fourth Grade Nothing* and drag it out over eight weeks while handing students answer comprehension question upon comprehension question. I share the story of Jack who was the first student ever to tell me to my face that reading "sucks," the conversation that ensued and how it has changed me as a teacher. I might share the story of Nathan, the most epic fake reader I have ever met. The point of these stories is not to self-indulge or simply wander down memory lane. This is a way for me to bring in my own reading identity, as well as my journey as a teacher. We have all made mistakes as teachers, especially as teachers of reading, but we have also grown from them, and it is this growth that I want students to understand. The next task is simple; on a post-it write down a reason why you have liked or disliked reading. Write as many post-its as you would like; one reason per post-it. Hang each post-it on the board. Book abandonment always comes up in this discussion as student after student will write that they hate reading because they were told to read a certain a book, because they had to finish a book they started. And so on that day, the second day of school, we take a huge step toward creating more passionate readers—I give them the power to abandon any book at any time for any reason.

Before students share out, I ask them to share in their table group. They guide the conversation and I simply listen in. It is always fascinating to me how similar the reasons are for why children end up disliking reading; no choice, no time, too many tasks when they finish a book, and "bad" books always come up multiple times. After a few minutes or when the conversation naturally dies down, we share out as a group. Students choose whether they want to start with likes or dislikes, and we discuss as a whole class. This simple post-it lesson, or even just discussion, is the cornerstone of our entire reading exploration for the year. This is when students start to think about how they identify as readers, where those identifiers come from, and whether they still have hope. I always tell them my secret—that the kids who really dislike reading are actually some of my favorite students. The reaction that this inspires in many of my most ardent anti-readers is amazing, "You mean, you actually like kids like me?" one boy exclaimed one year. Yes, I do, because a kid like him is one of the reasons I started on this journey to become a better English teacher. As the students pack up, the post-its stay up as a reminder as we start our reading journey together; this is an urgent journey and one that matters greatly, just look at all of these barriers there are to overcome.

Image 5.1 Students' post-its inspire our reading journey

The Emotions of Book Abandonment

This year I have learned to love reading and have learned what kinds of books I enjoy, and I've learned what kinds of books I do not enjoy. I have learned that the only way I will want to read is if I have good book, otherwise I need to abandon it.

—Kaitlyn, seventh grader

As mentioned earlier in the book, in the spring of 2016, I asked teachers across North America to have their students take a survey on book abandonment to see what students' thought process and emotions were when they abandoned books. More than 1,200 students ranging in age from 9 to 13 took it anonymously. While I expected a wide range of emotions to come up in the survey answers, I was taken aback by just how much guilt or disappointment in themselves or the book the students reported having from the act of abandonment. In fact, a whole slew of negative emotions came up for at least 400 of the students, or 33%, when asked how they felt about abandoning books. As one student wrote, "I feel unaccomplished and guilty [when I abandon a book]." Guilt constantly came up and how it was attached to the act of abandonment. Some reported feeling guilt toward the authors because they had tried to write a good book and now this student did not like it. One child wrote, "I feel that I am insulting the author and failing myself." Failing the teacher was another aspect of emotions attached to the act of abandonment, as one child said, "I feel kind of bad because the person or teacher that picked it for me wasted their time and I feel like they will be mad because I don't want to say, 'Here's your book back, it sucked.'" This speaks volumes to the emotional attachment humans have to books; we feel guilty when others take time to help us find a book and it does not work for us, we feel guilty when we dislike a book others may like, we even feel bad for the author because we did not like their book. Is it any wonder that many students associate more negative emotions with reading than positive ones? While I would rather have students who have an emotional attachment to the books they do or do not read, we have to take the emotion and turn it into a positive one. Because when a child writes, "I can't read that's what I think" when asked why he or she abandons a book, then we have the wrong kind of emotional investment. It is therefore imperative, as a step toward establishing healthy, positive student reading identities, that we change how book abandonment functions within our learning communities.

While many students reported that they felt a sense of relief as well when abandoning books, some even associated it with a positive state of emotions. As one child wrote, "When I abandon a book I feel good because then I can start another book and I don't have to read a book that I did not like! I also feel very powerful because I got to choose to put it down." Think of the power of this statement. Not only is this child delighted that he knows he can abandon a book, he also relishes the fact that he is now given an opportunity to find a better book for himself. This should matter to us as reading teachers; this is a child that feels in control of his reading experience, this is a child who will seek out other positive reading experiences outside of our learning community. The final part of the statement speaks to what book abandonment really is all about—the empowerment of students—and this child gets it. It is incredibly powerful to be allowed to choose whether to read a certain book or not. This is what can make or break a reader. Notice again that it is not a choice of *whether* to read, the choice is *which book* to read. And this is what carries us forward as passionate reading teachers; we must strive to create an environment where children feel validated in who they are as readers, while supported in expanding their repertoire, as well as their reading habits.

I wish I had realized this many years sooner, because the truth is, I did not listen to my own intuition. Instead, I followed the assumed protocol that I thought all teachers of reading followed. I did not change my policy, even though I saw what forcing children to stick with a book did to their reading lives. I did not change my policy even though I had a sneaking suspicion that the children who said they read many books outside of school really did not, even if the parent signature was on the reading log. I did not change my policy until I started to realize the damage that this book abandonment policy would have had on myself as a young reader. I was allowed to explore freely, to abandon wildly, and to always pursue my ever-changing interest in reading materials. I still embrace that luxury of a reading life, we all do as adults. So when 33% of the 1,200 students whom I surveyed about the feelings associated with abandoning a book told me that they felt guilty, sad, or disappointed in themselves, my heart sank. Reading should never be a guilt-filled experience, nor should it be one that causes more self-loathing in our students. It should never be something that makes our students feel bad. Knowing this, a major step we take to creating passionate reading environments is to tell students that if they do not like a book, let it go. That when they abandon a book, they should perhaps celebrate it at first; after all, this is a first step in knowing yourself as a reader. However, after a while, the act of abandoning should elicit no real response, instead it should just be seen as a natural part of being readers who know themselves, who know when a book does not work for them. We speak of "good fit" books in our learning communities and then forget that even the best readers will sometimes select books that do not work for them for whatever reason, and they then let that book go. For the survey, I surveyed my own students as well and loved many of their responses. When I asked how they felt about book abandonment, most replied similarly to this student, "I don't really think about it." And why should they? Knowing when to let a book go because it will harm your reading experience is equally as important as how to select the right book for you. Therefore, here are a few ideas for how you can create a passionate reading environment that embraces free book abandonment.

Share Your Own Abandonments

I celebrate my book abandoning because it tells the students that I am reader who knows herself. That I am tuned in to my own reading needs to find a book that works for me at that moment. And that those needs change depending on what is going on in my life. Students need an abandonment role model so that the stigma can be removed and the conversations can begin. Because that is what we need—more discussion. More reflection. I never tear a book apart. I instead explain why it is not a great fit for me right now, and then offer it up to others. Most of the time someone grabs it and proves me wrong.

Log It

No, not a reading log. I don't need to know minutes or pages read, but instead a list of books they have finished and books they have abandoned. They have a reader's notebook in our learning community that has a section for this so they can easily do it in class. Students need to have a way to examine their own actions, and so the simple sheet with the title on it helps them do just that, which leads to the next thing.

Ask Why

Assume that all students abandon books, not just the "bad" readers, and then ask them why they abandoned that book specifically. Have them examine their own habits so that they can figure out who they are as a reader. My students reflect on their reading habits several times a quarter so that they can see patterns. They look at their list of books they loved and books they didn't so they can get clues to what they like to read, and then start to pay attention to it. They need to study themselves and be given the time to do so, so they can learn from this rather than just view it as an inevitable part of their reading habits.

Ask "Now What?"

Too often, our students expect us to come up with the answer, to hand them the next book. I have learned that while we should support their book browsing, we also need to pull back to let them become "wild readers," as Donalyn Miller says, readers who know who they are and what they like. So when children abandon a book and ask me for another recommendation, I ask them to look at their to-be-read list, to think for a moment about what they need right now, what their life looks like, and how much energy they have. They then have to find a stack of books to browse through so they can find their next read. They usually let me know at the end what they pick, not because they have to, but because they want to share their find.

Practice Total Honesty

I ask my students to be completely honest about their reading habits, whether when we speak or when they reflect, because if they are not I cannot help them. They have to trust me to not punish them or somehow degrade their answers. And I don't. Total honesty is paramount to how we work in our learning community. And that starts with me; I do not sugarcoat my own habits. If I did not read the night before they know. If I am dragging in a book, they know. And they also know my reading goals because I set them right alongside theirs.

Ask Probing Questions

I will ask children the harder questions. I will ask them if they are just giving up because they are in a pattern of giving up. I will ask them if they think they should try a few more pages or if they have given it careful thought. That does not mean there are rules for when you abandon, but I do want to make sure that the decision to abandon is one that they know should be carefully considered. That yes, sometimes we know after one page that we do not want to read a book, and that is perfectly fine, as long as we know why we don't want to read it anymore.

Creating learning communities where students are passionate about reading requires many things—a great classroom library, time to read, choice, and also the courage to break some of the rules that surround traditional reading instruction. That includes facing book abandonment head on, but also creating shared reading experiences. Those moments that tie us together as a community of readers, not just as a learning community where reading is taught.

Questions to ponder as you reflect on your own book abandonment policies:

♦ When do you abandon a book?
♦ Do the students know which books they abandon?
♦ Do the students know why they are abandoning the books they are?
♦ What is the step after a child abandons a book?
♦ Do the students share their whole reading truth with you? How do you know?
♦ What questions can you ask when a child abandons a book?
♦ How can children use their abandonment history as a way to probe their own reading identity?

Component of Change: Reclaiming the Labels They Use

I hated reading. I thought I had much better things to be doing. I wasn't the fastest reader, I was actually pretty bad at reading. Now I am the total opposite. I like to read and I actually consider doing it sometimes. I read harder books now and I am much better at reading.

—Destany, seventh grader

Part of my conversation with students about their reading identity is listening for how they describe themselves. What terminology do they use to describe their reading habit and where do these terms come from? Few kids come to school thinking of themselves as bad readers, yet many kids leave school with that idea. So somewhere on their journey a label is either thrust upon them, concocted by themselves, or somehow attached to their personality through our reading instruction or intervention. This is so pervasive that once a label seems to have attached itself to a child, it can end up becoming one of their defining qualities and also becomes an identifier. We end up discussing our "struggling" readers as if they are one coherent group who share the same reading struggles, rather than the true diverse group of needs that the term represents. In our quest for more data to better understand the kids we teach, we can end up characterizing kids more by their perceived deficits than their strengths; after all, the data tells us all about them. Therefore, I have often found that discovering the language that students use to describe themselves can give us great insight to where on their reading journey they are. Students will sometimes label themselves as "bad" readers because they have received reading intervention (even if an interventionist never used that language or made them feel that way) or call themselves "slow" readers and say it like it is a bad thing. Other students might consider themselves good readers because they can read quickly or a test score has told them so. Because of these preconceived labels, I am careful with the labels I use in the classroom to classify readers. There are no "bad" readers, but only developing ones, because that is the truth; we are all developing as readers. There are no "nonreaders." Slow reading is changed to careful reading, and every single time we discuss our reading habits, these terms are used. In fact, one of the most common conversations we have, particularly at the beginning of the year, is how we must reclaim the notion of being a slow reader. This loaded term is something students whisper to me in reading conferences or hold up as evidence of why they are a "bad" reader. So a point I continue to make is, "Being a slow reader does not make you a bad reader!" because since when did taking your time as you read become something to be ashamed of?

Consequently, changing students' self-perception of who they are as readers, particularly when it is tinged with negativity, is not a one-slogan battle. We must therefore continue to give them an opportunity to talk about who they are as readers as they share their true reading lives throughout the year. When they tell us that being a slow reader means they hate reading, that they cannot find any books, that there is no way they will ever read enough books in seventh grade and that there is nothing to be done about it, we must take their words seriously. Especially when it comes to the notion of fast equals good reader, because this tells us that they have given up because of speed. They have given up because of everything they have attached to the word "slow." And with our emphasis on getting things done, including books, in our schools, I cannot blame them. So I tell them instead that they are not "slow," they are simply taking their time. That yes, increasing reading speed can become a goal for them, but that it should not be the only goal. That I understand that when you read at a slower pace (notice the difference in word choice) you sometimes lose meaning, so we need to find a pace that works for them. Because, you see, being a fast reader does not make you a great reader. In fact, I struggle publicly with my own fast reading and have as one of my goals that I need to slow down.

Yet, they do not believe me. Not yet anyway. And how can they? When the standardized tests they take to measure their worth as readers are timed. When the countdown clock appears, urging them to hurry up and answer or else it will count against them. When I give them all a book challenge of reading twenty-five books or more, and they automatically feel that is a mountain they cannot conquer. When they see their friends whizzing through books and cannot help but compare themselves. Once again it comes down to the choices we make as a reading community and what those choices signal to students. In our obsession with timed tests that can somehow measure reading skills, we have created environments where fast equals good and slow equals bad. But it is not too late to change this, it never is, no matter what tests we have to give our students or the groupings we are told to do. We still get to determine how we speak to our readers and how we can help them reshape the identity that they have. We can help them see their many facets as readers and help them reach the goals that they set for themselves.

As Thomas Newkirk says, "There is no ideal speed in reading" (2). Instead, it depends on the purpose, the time, the book they are reading, and sometimes even just their state of mind. So finding their comfortable speed in reading is what we should be teaching toward. In our instruction, we must leave opportunities for students to find a reading pace that works for them and then make sure that the reading environment we create supports that. We have to remove the stigma of the word "slow." We have to help our students find success as readers, to redefine their own reading identity so that

that very identity does not become a stranglehold or the reason they give up before they even begin. So we hand them books they can conquer successfully to build up the confidence they lack. And I don't mean books designated by levels, but books that they want to read based on interest. We hand them graphic novels. We hand them page-turners so they will want to read on. And then we hand them time. We remove the "get it done" pace that seems to surround us as we teach. And every time they say they are slow readers and mean it as a bad thing, we tell them they are mistaken. We change the language we use so that they can find a new way to identify themselves. So that they can feel proud of the time they take when they read, rather than see it as yet another deficit. We decide what being a slow reader means. That change comes from us. Our job is to make sure students know it. And our job is to make sure that students understand the labels they have chosen or have been given. What do they mean for the readers they are or who they would like to be? Uncover them, discuss them, and keep it as an ongoing cornerstone of their reading identity journey. Let them get the opportunity to end the year with a different notion of the labels they carry. As one student told me at the end of the year, "Mrs. Ripp, I am a slow reader but that is because I want to savor every word."

Questions to ponder as you reflect on the labels students give themselves:

◆ What are the labels your students use about themselves?
◆ What is the language you use when talking about readers?
◆ How are your students affected by your language choices?
◆ What "public" conversations should you have when it comes to the labels we use for ourselves?
◆ How can you support the reshaping of your students' labels?

This is why one of the biggest responsibilities we have is to offer a safe environment for students to explore their identity, no matter their age. To create an environment where students can relate to each other, even if their lives seem very different. To create an environment where all children can find out that they are good enough, that they are smart enough, that they are not broken. To create a community where all children are accepted, no matter their background, their race, their religion, or any other identifier that may shape their lives. We can do this through the books we place in our libraries, through the experiences we share as a reading community. Our classroom library spans age groups, it spans ability levels, and it spans topics that may not be suited for all but are certainly suited for some. Because the students I teach deserve to have classroom experiences that matter to who they are and what they believe in. Because the students I teach deserve to have a classroom experience that will allow them to feel found. Because they deserve to have book experiences that are not based on what I think they need, but rather on a myriad of books that may bring topics into their lives that they need to learn about, that they may already know about but no one else does. We teach children whose lives we can never imagine, who may go home to a life that looks nothing like the one we thought they had. We teach children who are curious by nature, whose curiosity may lead them down a path that is destructive unless we somehow find a way to warn them. We teach children who have so many questions about the bigger world but no idea how to answer them. Books help us reach these children. Our decisions about how we treat every single child in our day-to-day routine help us reach all children. Each experience that we have with the children we are fortunate to teach is one that will shape their adult decisions when it comes to whether they see themselves as readers or not. So the labels we place on children today can be labels that they carry with them for many years to come. The labels that we place on children today may be labels that they tell their own children about some day. May we never forget that we do not just teach this generation of children, but their future children as well, as they pass on the values we helped them discover. May we remember that we do not just teach children, we also teach the unwritten history of our world.

Questions to ponder as you reflect on developing student reading identity:

◆ How do the students identify on their reading journey? How do you know?
◆ Who leads the reading journeys in your learning community?
◆ How can more emphasis be placed on student autonomy within your curriculum?
◆ How are reading goals set now and reflected upon?
◆ Do you know where each child is on his or her reading journey?

My love of reading never had to survive my childhood. My love of reading never had to survive well-meaning teachers, at least not when I was young. When I grew up, teachers weren't really that bothered with what we read, or how much we read every night, just that we read. That we grew. That we became better. They didn't ask us to keep logs, to record minutes, to stick post-it notes whenever we had a thought to make sure we could turn and talk about the amazing thing we just connected with. They didn't tell us which box to pick from or even give us a label. Instead, they gave us a book, pointed to a chair, and they told us to read. Come up for air when you are done, and I'll hand you another book.

Some may shudder at the lack of instruction that I was put through as a young child, after all, where was all of the teaching? And yet within this brutally simplistic approach—read, read, read and then please read some more—was an immense amount of wisdom. Kids need time to read. We know that. Kids need choice. Kids need to be allowed to self-select books, and then when they are done reading, they should be asked to go have a conversation and get another book, not fill out a packet. So if we hold these truths to be self-evident, I wonder, how has so much of our reading instruction gotten so far off track?

I think we teachers are part of the problem. I know I am. I think our silence while we seethe inside at the new initiatives being dictated to us means that we are now complicit in the killing of the love of reading. For too long we have been too nice, unwilling to rock the boat too much, because that is what we do as teachers. We have sat idly by for too long as others have told us that students will love reading more if we limit them further and guide them more. We have held our tongues while practices have been marched into our classrooms disguised by words like research-based, rigorous, and common-core aligned. We have held our tight smiles as experts sold our districts more curriculum, more things to do, more interventions, more repetitions. We have stayed silent because we were afraid of how our words would be met, and I cannot blame any of us.

Standing up and speaking out is terrifying, especially if you are speaking out against something within your own district. But we cannot afford to stay silent any more. With the onslaught of more levels, more logs, more things to do with what they read all in the name of deeper understanding, we have to speak up. Because as we know reading is about time to read first. About falling in love with a book. About creating a personal connection with something that is inherently yours. Not all of the other things. So if we are sacrificing time to read to instead teach children more strategies, then we are truly missing the point of what we should be doing.

So I declare myself a reading warrior, and I believe you should as well. No more reading logs to check whether kids are reading. No more levels used to stop children from self-selecting books they actually want to read. No more timed standardized tests to check for comprehension. Being a fast reader does not mean you are a good reader. No more reading projects that have nothing to do with reading. No more reading packets to produce a grade that stops students from actually talking about the books they have read. No more rewards: prizes, stickers, lunches with the principal. We cannot measure a great reader by how many pages a school has read, so stop publishing it. Don't publish your test scores. Don't publish your AR levels. Publish instead how many children have fallen in love with a book. How many recommendations have been made from student to student. Publish how many books have needed to be replaced because of worn pages. Publish that, and be proud of the teachers that dare to speak up to protect the very thing we say we hold sacred. Create environments where these teachers are supported, where reading is embedded and students' love of reading is protected.

So become a reading warrior, because for too long we have hoped that the decisions being made are always in the best interest of a child when we know at times they are not. Become a reading warrior because we have been quiet for too long. Become a reading warrior because our children deserve someone who fights for them. No child is helped when we protest in silence, in the teacher lounge, or behind closed doors. We have to find the courage to speak up for the very students we serve. We have to practice being brave. We have to allow students to read books that they choose, to give them time to talk about their books rather than fill out a packet, and to allow them to self-monitor how much reading they are doing and then believing them when they tell us their truth. It is time for us to stand up and speak up.

It is time to take back our reading instruction and truly make it about what the kids need and not what others tell us that they need. One voice can be a whisper or a protest; we make the choice when we decide to make a difference. Are you with me?

Component of Change: The Reading Identity Challenge

By mid-year, through a lot hard work, a lot of book talks, a lot of time to read, and a lot of perseverance, many of the students I teach are typically reading more. Not everyone, but a good majority of children are having more positive experiences with text and have moved at least a little on the scale from hating reading to having a more positive disposition toward it. Yet, I know how easy it is to lose those better reading habits once we, the teachers, and the community we have created are no longer an everyday presence. So how do we continue to build on the experience we create while gradually releasing the responsibility over to the students?

One of the components I have used more recently is the reading identity challenge; a challenge meant to not just help the kids who still hate reading midway through, but also for all the kids who need a spark and those who need to stretch their reading legs a little. So, in essence, all of the students we teach. This reading challenge centers around the notion of all of us being challenged to become better readers, whatever being a better reader means for us. The concept is simple—over the course of three or four weeks, depending on the students, they will select one aspect of their personal reading life and challenge themselves to either change that one area or somehow strengthen it. Much like a personal goal, there is no right challenge. Instead, it is based on the needs of every individual child and their hopes for a better reading future. There is no limit as to what they can work on, as long as the goal is tied in with reading and is meaningful to them. Every day, for the three or four weeks the challenge runs, students are given extra reading time, up to 25 minutes rather than our normal 10.

To kick off the reading challenge, we start with the five-page reading identity challenge survey found in the appendix. Yes, five pages. I need students in all the stages of their reading relationship to uncover new truths about themselves. So the survey is crafted to go beyond the standard questions such as "What do you like to read? How much do you read and where do you find books?" to include, hopefully, areas that they perhaps have not considered yet for their reading identity. Questions such as where are they reading, why are they not reading more, what are genres they avoid and why, and who are their reading buddies? All are questions meant to make them see the bigger picture of who they really are as readers, since all of these little things play into the formation of their reading identity. While the survey, due to its length, takes almost two days for students to fill out completely and thoroughly, it is worth every minute invested. I ask the students to slow down, really think about it, and then finally I ask them to show me their goal so that I can approve it for them. Approval hinges on whether it is actually a challenging goal for them or not.

The goals always vary, which is what is meant to happen. I want to enjoy reading again, I want to try a new genre, I want to read every day, and I want to recommend books are all goals I have seen and approved. When children cannot think of a goal, we go through their survey to find an area that will work for them. The goal needs to be meaningful to students and also help them create a better relationship with reading. I rarely do not give approval of the goals; after all, these goals are meant to be personal and so they each have a personal reason for pursuing their goal. Due to many kids wanting to have an enjoyable experience, I have been able to recruit adults to do a shared read-aloud with groups of students in some classes. Sometimes, this shared read-aloud is the very first book they complete all year.

For every goal there is always a story; a story of reading blossomed or reading gone wrong. For every goal there is excitement or slight reprehension— how will this challenge actually change anything?—but I tell the students to have faith and to commit to the challenge. Once all goals are in place, I ask the students to somehow keep track of their goal progress. Some choose to keep a self-created reading journal or calendar, some choose to reflect via various social media tools, and some simply do minor check-ins with me or peers. I do not want this to turn into a "write about your daily reading" type of activity, because so many of my students have told me how much they detest this type of work, and so again, I ask my students to carefully think about how they can keep track in a way that is meaningful to them.

As we begin, some kids already know which book they will read and others book shop for a while, sometimes up to two days. These are often the kids whose goals tie in with actually liking reading more. Once everyone has a book and is settled into the process, I will start every class with a short whole lesson and then release them to read, much like the regular workshop model. I pull mini lesson groups to work on separate skills, such as reading comprehension strategies, or I do one-on-one conferring with students as they read. These few weeks offer me a chance to review the work that needs to be reviewed or even teach more in-depth to some groups of kids that need it.

What I have noticed from the reading identity challenge is that success varies from child to child. While one child may have discovered that a detested genre may have great books to offer after all, another child may finally have read more than ten pages in a day. The measures of success are so different from child to child, because the children we teach and their reading identities are so different. Whatever their goal is, I see the small changes happening gradually— most kids finding a way to take control of their reading lives and to make reading better for themselves. While the reading identity challenge is not the be all and end all, it is another step in helping students uncover unknown or forgotten aspects of who they are as readers. It is another tool to help them become empowered in their own reading journey. It is another step to tell all of our students that reading matters and that they control so much of their relationship with reading. That new genres await, that it is possible for reading to be enjoyable, that they can make it through the boring parts of a book, that they can go deeper in their text. That reading should be a part of who they are and therefore also should be something they mold and shape as they develop further.

Questions to ponder as you plan for your own reading identity challenge:

◆ When would a challenge like this fit in with your curriculum?
◆ Which mini-lessons could you review or teach deeper through a unit like this?
◆ How can you support students in creating meaningful goals?
◆ What could your own goals be since you should challenge yourself as well?
◆ What would you hope students would get out of a challenge like this?

In the End: Maintaining Hope for Our Students and Our Mission

Reading is basically an art.

—Adam C., seventh grader

I was born a reader, it seems, surrounded by books, with free choice and plenty of time to read under my covers with a flashlight. I was shaped as a reader in the conversations I had with my family and friends, spurred on by their self-knowledge to embark on my own reading journey, knowing that I would never be judged by my choices and instead would be encouraged to roam free with a book under my arm, ready to read at a moment's notice. I shape the reading lives of our future generations of children through the small decisions and choices I make every single day in our learning community together. I can be the reason a child loves to read or hates it for the rest of their life, and so can you. The weight of that is what drove me to write this book. The words my students have shared demanded to be shared with the rest of the world so others could learn from their truths. We are in urgent need of better reading experiences in our schools, not just to drive up test scores, but to help children become adults who read. To help our children have experiences in our learning communities that support them to become the best human beings they possibly can be, no matter their previous experiences in school and with reading, no matter their start in life.

On December 19, 2013, our youngest daughter, Augustine, was born almost 10 weeks early. She came so fast that there was no doctor in the room, just the nurse. She came so fast that I now know what the big red emergency button in a hospital room does. She came so fast that I did not see her. I did not hold her. She did not cry. For the first minute of her life, I did not know if she was alive. It wasn't until my husband, Brandon, told me she was breathing that I think I took a breath. That life started up again because for that longest minute of my life, with no wailing to calm me down, I had no idea if I was still the mother of three or now the mother of four.

They whisked her away from me into their machines, into the equipment that would help her tiny body breathe and stay warm and her heart keep beating. See, when babies are born that early, they need help with everything. And we can prepare all we want, but it is not until they actually arrive and we see how much they need us that we realize that all of a sudden we have started a new journey, one that will take us down a perilous path where we might not be able to see our destination for a long time.

In the week leading up to her much-too-soon arrival, I was in the hospital waiting. Willing my body to slow down. We were not ready. She was not ready. One night a doctor from the NICU visited me to help me prepare for what would happen in case she came. His words have stuck with me all of this time. He said, "When she comes we will be ready. We will have the machines that will help her breathe. We will have the machines that will keep her warm. We will monitor her heart and we will be by your side. We will do everything in our power to keep her alive, to keep her safe, to help her no matter what. While we can help her with her needs, we will not know about her brain. We will not know what long-term effects being born so early will have on her learning. We will not know if her brain will be damaged, we will not know until she grows, until she reaches her milestones. We will not know what her future path will look like when it comes to learning but we will be ready. We will be by her side because that is what we do." That is what we do . . .

As I held Augustine for the very first time more than 24 hours later, I held all of our dreams for her as well. As we sat in the quiet, listening to the alarms and the beeps on her monitor, I knew that her future was now in my hands as well, and that all we could do now was our best. That all we could do now was to be by her side and hope that her future teachers would see her for the miracle she is and not just a child who might have difficulties learning. That reading, or math, or even sitting still and focusing might become a struggle. We simply would not know until she grew.

The hopes we carry for our own children are much like the hopes we carry for the students we teach. Every year as the new year awaits, these students arrive in all of their glory. They arrive with all of their dreams, their hopes, and their needs. They show up whether we are ready or not. And so we prepare, we plan, we dream over the summer that this will be the year that we reach every single child we teach. That every child that comes to us will give us a chance, will give reading a chance, and will find a space in our learning communities that they can call home.

We do not pick who we teach. We do not pick who shows up. We do not pick who these kids are that we are supposed to have life-changing experiences with, but instead we stand by our doors like the Statue of Liberty and say, "Give me your tired, your poor, your huddled masses yearning to breathe free . . ."

We can prepare all we want as teachers. We can create learning communities where most of our students will thrive. We can plan for fictitious children and hope they will fit into the boxes we create. Or we can teach the kids that come. We can create experiences that center on the kids who actually show up instead of the kids we hope to teach. Teaching literacy offers us one of the greatest opportunities to not just get to know our students, but also to help them become the human being they hope to be. In our reading experiences, we can help students discover who they are and who they want to be. We can open our classroom doors wide to make sure that all children who enter, that all children who show up, know that with us they will learn, with us they will read, with us they will matter. Because they do. And we can ask those kids how we can be the types of teachers they need. We can ask those kids how they would like to learn and then we can listen to their truths and become the teachers they need.

So we can take them all and we can love them all because that is the least we can do. We work tirelessly every day so that those kids who become our kids know that with us they belong, that with us it does not matter what their start in life was because in here they have a chance at success. That with us it does not matter whether they were born 10 weeks early, don't have a good home life, or have never liked school. That with us all that matters is that they showed up. That we are here to listen, that we are here to teach, that we are here to create reading experiences that extend beyond the to-do and instead become the to-be.

Augustine did not ask to be born early; she did not ask to have such a hard start in her life. She did not ask to have a harder path than our other kids. The kids that come to us with their broken dreams and their battered hearts didn't ask for that either. Didn't ask to have a different life than so many others. So our job is to teach. Is to love. Is to be by their side. Is to listen to their reading truths and do something about the things they tell us. To help them see that with us their reading identity will be protected, shaped, and nurtured.

Last summer, as Augustine went to her NICU checkup appointment, we heard the sweetest words: "Your daughter is perfectly average." While her path is still unwinding and we are not in the clear just yet, we see hope with every word she learns, every task she accomplishes. We see her for the miracle she truly is, a child who would not have lived not too many years ago. So may we all see the miracle that is the child who enters our schools. May we all know just how lucky we are to teach these kids, even when our days are long and our lesson plans are broken. Even when we feel we are not enough, may we still try.

As teachers, we were never promised it would be easy. We were never promised that our jobs would be effortless. Or that our hearts would stay protected. But we were told that it would be worth it. That this may be one of the hardest jobs and yet also the most rewarding. So every day as we welcome the kids, make sure it is every child we welcome, not just the easy ones, the ones that barely need us. Make sure your learning community is a place for any child to succeed, not just with reading but with whatever you teach, no matter their start in life. Because much like the NICU doctor told me more than three years ago—we are ready, we are here, and we will stay here until you no longer need us. It is the very least we can do.

As teachers of reading, we are not always given the most time, the best books, or students who already love reading, but we cannot let those components stand in our way. We can create incredible learning experiences for our students that will transform their reading identities, but to do so we must start to look at the components that we use that may harm their love of reading. We must look at our own choices and practices to see what role we play. For in the end, what mattered was not just what we taught all of the children, but the very experiences we created. May your learning community be filled with passionate readers for all the days to come.

Appendix

Name _____

Tell Us a Little Bit About Yourself

Do you have access to a computer with internet at home? _____

Do you have a device such as a smartphone to bring to school? _____

How do you get to and from school? _____

Describe what your typical afternoon looks like after school

_____

_____

_____

What are three important things I should know about you?

_____

_____

_____

What are some things you are really good at?

_____

_____

_____

What have you most loved learning about or to do (even if not in school)?
Why?

_____

_____

_____

I think 7th grade will be . . . (write as much as you would like)

_____

_____

_____

What do you love about school?

_____

_____

_____

What do you not like so much about school?

_____

_____

_____

I work best in a classroom that is . . .

_____

_____

_____

Some things I really want to work on this year in 7th grade are . . .

_____

_____

_____

What do you wish teachers would notice about you?

_____

_____

_____

When I get mad, I . . . _____

_____

The best teachers for me are teachers that . . .

_____

_____

I do not get along with these students . . . _____

I work well with these students . . . _____

I wish all teachers would just . . . . _____

Name: _____   Number of books read: _____

Reading Habit Self-Reflection

We are 6 weeks into the year. It is time for us to reflect on our reading habits so far. Please be honest rather than write what you think I want to hear.

How much time do you spend reading every day? _____

Favorite book so far this year? _____

Do you read every day? Why or why not? _____
_____
_____

Do you like to read? Why or why not? _____
_____
_____

Are you using the reading comprehension strategies when you read? _____ **If yes, how has it helped you?** _____

If no, why not?
_____

What is a good habit you have as a reader? _____
_____

What is a bad habit you have as a reader and how will you work on it?
_____
_____

How many books do you think you have abandoned in the past 6 weeks? _____ **If any, what made you abandon them?** _____
_____
_____

What are you working on as a reader? _____
_____
_____

How will you work on this? _____
_____
_____

What do you wish I would notice?
_____
_____
_____

The 25 (At Least) Book Challenge*

Welcome to the 25 book challenge! In 7th grade, you are expected to read at least 25 books. If you already know you will read at least 25 books, I would like you to set a higher goal than that which we will do in class.

How are books counted:

- Books with more than 300 pages count as 2 books, books with more than 500 pages count as 3 books. More than 800 pages—see Mrs. Ripp.
- Graphic novels count as 1/4, 1/2, or 1 whole book, depending in the book.
- Audiobooks count as 1 book.

Further details:

- You pick the books you want to read.
- You have until the end of the year.
- You are only competing against yourself as a reader (and Mrs. Ripp if you want).
- 15 of the books must be actual chapter books.
- This is meant to push you as a reader. If 25 is too little of a goal for you, please set a higher goal. My goal will be 85 books.

How do you record it:

There are many ways to record your 25 books. Here are a few examples:

- You can use Goodreads
- You can use Padlet
- You can use a Google Docs
- You can come up with your own idea
- You can use the in-class all year reader's notebook (provided)

*Inspired by The 40 Book Challenge created by Donalyn Miller, see https://bookwhisperer.com/2014/08/12/the-40-book-challenge-revisited/

Dear Parent(s) or Guardian(s),

Think back to the last time you were trying to find a book to read—which book did you choose to read? Why did you want to read that particular book? All of us have different reading lives, and all of us enjoy reading different genres, titles, or authors. I find that to be true with my students as well, which is why I have an extensive classroom library with thousands of books available for them to check out. Since loving reading and books is one of the major goals of our year together in English, our classroom library plays a major role in the pursuit of that.

One of the things I love about teaching seventh graders is just how unique they are. The differences in student interests and maturity levels, as well as learning goals, are vast and varied. These kids are not only different ages; they arrive at school with different reading levels, different backgrounds, and different experiences that have shaped their lives in both positive and negative ways. They therefore have different needs when it comes to reading. As a teacher, I have a responsibility to serve all of the kids who come to me, and a responsibility to offer literature choices that speak to all of them.

Kids, in general, do a fantastic job of self-selecting books, and when they find they've picked up something they're not ready for, they're usually quick to put it down and ask for help choosing something else. (In fact, I encourage my students to abandon books that are not right for them at that time.) As a teacher, I'll offer recommendations and steer kids toward books that are age and individually appropriate, however, self-selecting a book is a pillar of our reading community.

As a teacher, I respect your right to help your own child choose reading material, and ask that you respect the rights of other parents/guardians to do the same. If you object to your child reading a particular book, let me know, send it back, and I'll help your child find another selection. I'll put the first book back on the shelf, because even though you don't feel it's the right book for your child right now, it may be the perfect book for someone else's child. I would also encourage you to speak to your child about what types of books he or she feels comfortable reading so that this becomes a part of his or her selection process as well. If I can ever be of help to you in recommending titles for your family, please don't hesitate to ask.

Our library will have a wide range of choices for kids—to meet all of their varied needs and help them all develop an appreciation of reading. This includes our picture book selection that spans many social and historical issues. These are used for mini lessons throughout the year as a way to garner discussion and reflection on our role as human beings. Through the use of these shared read-alouds, I hope for students to love reading and storytelling. Please feel free to reach out if you have any questions or would like to visit our classroom library. Finally, thank you for your involvement in your child's education and helping to encourage reading growth and engagement.

Sincerely,
Pernille Ripp

*Adapted and modified from a letter created by Kate Messner at *www.katemessner.com/heading-off-book-challenges/*

Name:

Date:	Book Reading:
Observation: Now What?	What are you working on as reader?

Date:	Book Reading:
Observation: Now What?	What are you working on as reader?

Date:	Book Reading:
Observation: Now What?	What are you working on as reader?

Standard	Official language
ELA 1:	Determine/analyze development of central ideas/themes in a text.
ELA 2:	Analyze how story elements interact.
ELA 3:	Write informative texts to convey ideas; select, organize, and analyze content; summarize.
ELA 4:	Write narratives to share real events, using vivid detail and ordered sequence.
ELA 5:	Draw evidence from texts to support written analysis.
ELA 6:	Command the conventions of standard English grammar, usage, and vocabulary.
ELA 7:	Present focused claims with support, using eye contact, volume, and elocution.

What Is My Reading Identity?

Your Early Reading Life

What is your earliest memory of reading?
How was reading a part of your childhood?
What are three books that stand out to you from your childhood reading life and why?
Did you have any reading role models in your childhood?
What were pleasurable experiences you had with reading in school?
What are experiences that you did not like with reading in school?
How have your earliest reading experiences shaped how you teach reading now?

Your Adult Reading Life

How much time do you spend reading for pleasure?
How do you select a book to read?
What are your favorite genres or authors?
Do you read children's books? Why or why not?
Do you set reading goals?
What are your book gaps?
Which five words would you use to describe your own reading life?

Your Reading Life in Your Classroom

Do your students know your reading habits?
What is the last book you book talked in school?
How do you incorporate book talks currently?
Which colleagues do you talk books with?
What does your classroom library say about you?
How do students have choice in what they read in your classroom?
How do students have choice in what they do with their reading in your classroom?

The Changes You Want to Pursue

Looking at your own reading life, what is the one thing you want to change right now?
How will you accomplish this?
Looking at your classroom reading philosophy, what is the one thing you want to change right now for your students?
How will you accomplish this?
Looking at your classroom set up, what is the one thing you want to change right now for your students?
How will you accomplish this?
What is one long-term change you want to work toward? How will you get there?

Name: _____   **Hour:** _____

End of Semester Student Reflection and Survey

How would you describe this class to someone that is not in it?
What was your favorite project or thing we have done so far?
What is your least favorite project or thing we have done so far?
How would you describe Mrs. Ripp to someone that does not have her as a teacher?
Is this a good class for you? Why or why not?
Do you like the way Mrs. Ripp teaches? Why or why not?
Do you get enough help in English?
What do you wish we would do more of (besides reading)?
What do you wish we would do less of?

What should Mrs. Ripp change in the way she teaches?
How many books have you read so far for your book challenge?
What are 3 goals that you have for the next semester in English? 1. 2. 3.
How will you accomplish each of those goals? 1. 2. 3.
What do you wish Mrs. Ripp would notice?
What is your advice on how we should do book clubs?
Anything else?

Name _____

Student End of Year Questionnaire:
Please be honest in your answers

Was this a good class for you? Why or why not?

```
┌─────────────────────────────────────────────┐
│                                             │
│                                             │
│                                             │
└─────────────────────────────────────────────┘
```

Did you like the way Mrs. Ripp teaches?

```
┌─────────────────────────────────────────────┐
│                                             │
│                                             │
│                                             │
└─────────────────────────────────────────────┘
```

How would you describe Mrs. Ripp to a friend?

```
┌─────────────────────────────────────────────┐
│                                             │
│                                             │
│                                             │
└─────────────────────────────────────────────┘
```

Was 7th grade a good year for you? Why or why not?

```
┌─────────────────────────────────────────────┐
│                                             │
│                                             │
│                                             │
└─────────────────────────────────────────────┘
```

Did you feel respected by Mrs. Ripp? Why or why not?

```
┌─────────────────────────────────────────────┐
│                                             │
│                                             │
│                                             │
└─────────────────────────────────────────────┘
```

Did you get enough help?

```
┌─────────────────────────────────────────────┐
│                                             │
│                                             │
│                                             │
└─────────────────────────────────────────────┘
```

Which project/task did you enjoy the most?

Which project/task should Mrs. Ripp never make 7th graders do?

What do you wish we had done more of?

What do you wish we had done less of?

What should Mrs. Ripp change in her classroom setup (how the classroom looks)?

What should Mrs. Ripp change in how she teaches?

What is the one thing you are always going to remember from this class?

Name: _____

End of Year Reading Survey

How were you as a reader at the beginning of the year?

_____

_____

_____

_____

_____

_____

How are you as a reader now?

_____

_____

_____

_____

_____

_____

How did this year help you grow as a reader?

_____

_____

_____

_____

_____

Over =======>

How did I, as your teacher, help you as a reader?

_____
_____
_____
_____
_____
_____

What do you wish every teacher would do for you as a reader?

_____
_____
_____
_____
_____
_____

What else could I, as your teacher, have done for you?

_____
_____
_____
_____
_____
_____

What type of books should our classroom have more of?

What other book bins should our classroom have?

How Are You as a Reader?

This is not for you to impress me, but rather to be honest about yourself so that I can help you have a great year!

Name: _____

Complete the sentences:

Reading is _____

_____

I read best when I _____

_____

Reading is hard when I _____

_____

I read because _____

_____

Reading in school would be even better if . . . _____

_____

_____

If you had to guess

How many books do you think you own? _____

How many books did you read in 6th grade? _____

How many books did you read over the summer? _____

Now, let's discuss your reading habits

1. What is your favorite thing to read? _____

_____

2. What do you read besides books? _____

_____

3. How do you decide what you will read next? _____

_____

4. Where do you typically get your books from? _____

_____

5. Do you read outside of English class? Why or why not?

_____

6. Would you consider yourself a slow, average, or fast reader—why?

_____

7. Would you consider yourself a bad, average, or good reader—why?

_____

8. What would you like to work on as a reader this year?

_____

_____

_____

_____

9. What else should I know about you?

_____

_____

_____

_____

_____

_____

Our Classroom Library Organization

Major Genres and Format

- ◆ Biography
- ◆ Fantasy
- ◆ Free Verse Novels
- ◆ Graphic Novels
- ◆ Historical Fiction
- ◆ Nonfiction
- ◆ Poetry
- ◆ Realistic Fiction
- ◆ Scary
- ◆ Science Fiction

Subgenres and classifications:

- ◆ Animal Fantasy
- ◆ Animals
- ◆ Crime
- ◆ Death and Dying
- ◆ Dystopian Science Fiction
- ◆ Fairytale Inspired
- ◆ Hero's Quest
- ◆ High School Experience
- ◆ J.K. Rowling
- ◆ Learn Something
- ◆ Life Stories
- ◆ Magical Fantasy
- ◆ Mystery
- ◆ Nature and Survival
- ◆ Personal Struggles
- ◆ Realistic Fantasy
- ◆ Rick Riordan
- ◆ Science and Space
- ◆ Social Justice
- ◆ Sports
- ◆ True Tales
- ◆ War History
- ◆ World War II

Subgenres are added as needed and removed when they are not being utilized much.

Reader Profile Quarter 1 for : _____

Initial Interview

Identifies self as a reader? ❏ Yes ❏ Not yet ❏ Not sure _____

Reads because? ❏ Loves to read ❏ Required to ❏ Other _____

Reads books outside of school? ❏ Yes ❏ No ❏ Sometimes—What? _____

Finds books to read via . . . ❏ School ❏ Library ❏ Recommendations ❏ Home ❏ Store ❏ Other

Reads independently in class? ❏ Every day ❏ Most days ❏ Sometimes ❏ When prompted ❏ No

Identifies speeds of reading as . . . ❏ Fast ❏ Average ❏ Slow ❏ Depends on book

Identifies as what type of reader? ❏ Good ❏ Average ❏ Bad ❏ Depends on book

Sticks with books? ❏ Most ❏ Depends on books ❏ Frequent abandonment

Reading identity based on: ❏ Teacher ❏ Self ❏ Grades/tests ❏ Unclear

Assessment Spring _____ Assessment Fall _____ Books read previous grade? _____

End of 1st Quarter Interview

What are you proud of this quarter? _____

Biggest goal right now? _____

What type of reader are you? _____

Reads because? ❏ Loves to read/Fun ❏ Required to ❏ Other _____

Reads books outside of school? ❏ Yes ❏ No Sometimes—How many days a week? _____

Selects next book by . . . _____

Reads independently in class? ❏ Every day ❏ Most days ❏ Sometimes ❏ When prompted ❏ No

Identifies speeds of reading as . . . ❏ Fast ❏ Average ❏ Slow/Careful ❏ Depends on book Why? _____

Identifies as what type of reader? ❏ Good ❏ Average ❏ Bad/Developing ❏ Depends on book

Sticks with books? ❏ Most ❏ Depends on books ❏ Frequent abandonment

Uses reading strategies in class? ❏ Knows them and uses them ❏ Knows them/no use ❏ Forgets ❏ Hard to tell

Most helpful thing this quarter? _____

What do you want me to tell your parents about you? _____

Goal for the year? _____ Books read? _____

Favorite Book (s) _____

Why? _____

End of 2nd Quarter Interview

What are you proud of this quarter? _____

Biggest goal right now? _____

What type of reader are you? _____

Reads because? ❑ Loves to read/Fun ❑ Required to ❑ Other _____

Reads books outside of school? ❑ Yes ❑ No ❑ Sometimes—How
many days a week _____

Selects next book by . . . _____

Reads independently in class? ❑ Every day ❑ Most days ❑ Sometimes ❑ When prompted ❑ No

Identifies speeds of reading as . . . ❑ Fast ❑ Average ❑ Slow/Careful ❑ Depends on book Why? _____

Identifies as what type of reader? ❑ Good ❑ Average ❑ Bad/Developing ❑ Depends on book

Sticks with books? ❑ Most ❑ Depends on books ❑ Frequent abandonment

Uses reading strategies in class? ❑ Knows them and uses them ❑ Knows them/no use ❑ Forgets
❑ Hard to tell

Most helpful thing this quarter? _____

What do you want me to tell your parents about you? _____

Goal for the year? _____ Books read? _____

Favorite Book (s) _____

Why? _____

End of 3rd Quarter Interview

What are you proud of this quarter? _____

Biggest goal right now? _____

What type of reader are you? _____

Reads because? ❑ Loves to read/Fun ❑ Required to ❑ Other _____

Reads books outside of school? ❑ Yes ❑ No ❑ Sometimes—How many days a week _____

Selects next book by . . . _____

Reads independently in class? ❑ Every day ❑ Most days ❑ Sometimes ❑ When prompted ❑ No

Identifies speeds of reading as . . . ❑ Fast ❑ Average ❑ Slow/Careful ❑ Depends on book Why? _____

Identifies as what type of reader? ❑ Good ❑ Average ❑ Bad/Developing ❑ Depends on book

Sticks with books? ❑ Most ❑ Depends on books ❑ Frequent abandonment

Uses reading strategies in class? ❑ Knows them and uses them ❑ Knows them/no use ❑ Forgets
❑ Hard to tell

Most helpful thing this quarter? _____

What do you want me to tell your parents about you? _____

Goal for the year? _____ Books read? _____

Favorite Book (s) _____

Why? _____

Name: _____   Class _____

Final Product	I don't really need help on this	I would like to check in with the teacher	I would like to work with a peer on this (If yes, who?)	I would like to be in a small group for this	I am not sure yet
One to Two Paragraph Summary					
Annotate the articles					
Constructed Response Opinion Piece (One whole-class lesson will be provided)					

Name: _____   Class _____

Final Product	I don't really need help on this	I would like to check in with the teacher	I would like to work with a peer on this (If yes, who?)	I would like to be in a small group for this	I am not sure yet
One to Two Paragraph Summary					
Annotate the articles					
Constructed Response Opinion Piece (One whole-class lesson will be provided)					

Uncovering Your Reading Identity

This reflection process is for you to help you uncover who you are as a reader. This is so you can figure out which facet of your reading life you would like to challenge yourself on over the course of the next several weeks. You will use the information uncovered here to help you set your own personal challenge goal or goals. Please answer truthfully this is not assessed or shared with anyone but me.

How many books have you read so far this year? _____

How far are you from your goal (25 books or higher)? _____

Is your year goal attainable? Why or why not? _____

_____

Your Own Reading Behaviors

On a scale from 1 to 10, how much do you like reading
(1—not at all, 10—I love it!) _____

Why is this your rating? _____

_____

_____

Has your rating changed this year? Why or why not? _____

_____

_____

Do you consider yourself a slow, average, or fast reader? _____

Why do you think this is your speed? _____

_____

Does your speed of reading help you or hinder you? _____

_____

When you read aloud, do you use expression? _____

What do you usually do during our independent reading time? _____

_____

_____

How many books do you think you have abandoned so far this year? _____

_____

_____

Think of the last book you abandoned; why did you abandon this book? _____

_____

_____

How has abandoning books helped you as a reader? _____

_____

_____

How has abandoning books hurt you as a reader? _____

_____

_____

Habits of Reading Outside of English

How many days on average do you read outside of English?_____

When you read, how long do you read for? _____

Where do you typically read? _____

Why this spot? _____

_____

_____

What stops you from reading more? _____

_____

_____

How much do you wish you were reading outside of English? _____

Why this amount? _____

Reading Habits of Others in Your Life

Do people at your home read? If yes—who? _____

Do you share book recommendations with your family? _____

Does your family read together? _____

Do your friends read? _____

How often do you share book recommendations with others? _____

What was the last book you recommended to someone else? _____

_____

Why did you recommend this book? _____

_____

If you do not recommend books to others, why not? _____

_____

_____

Your Own Reading Preferences

List your favorite types/formats of books (Picture books, graphic novels, free verse, chapter novels, etc.)

_____

_____

List your favorite genres of books _____

_____

_____

What are genres that you do NOT read? _____

_____

_____

Why do you not read these? _____

_____

_____

What is the hardest book that you have read this year and why was it hard? _____

_____

_____

What is a book you would like to still read this year and why? _____

_____

_____

Who is a favorite book character? Why this character? _____

_____

_____

Describe a time when reading was fun for you. _____

_____

_____

Describe a time when reading was NOT fun for you—why not? _____

_____

_____

PHEW! Now let's see what you may want to challenge yourself on.

Looking over all of these questions, which answers stand out to you? Why these? Self-reflect, speak to Mrs. Ripp on the answers you have given, and start to think of a goal or goals you may want to try for within the next several weeks.

Potential goal _____

_____

_____

Why this goal? _____

_____

_____

How will this goal challenge you? (Note: the goal should be attainable but not easy) _____

_____

_____

Who will hold you accountable to this challenge? _____

_____

_____

What are the mini-goals you can reach along the way?

1. _____

2. _____

3. _____

4. _____

How will you know you have succeeded? _____

_____

_____

How will you reward yourself when you reach your goal? _____

_____

_____

Works Cited

"Adding Ten Minutes of Reading Time Dramatically Changes Levels of Print Exposure." *Journal of Neurology, Neurosurgery & Psychiatry* 80.11 (2009): n. pag. *Educator's Briefing*. Scientific Learning, Mar. 2008. Web. 08 Nov. 2015.

Allington, Richard L. "The Six Ts of Effective Elementary Literacy Instruction." *Reading Rockets*. n. pag., n.d. Web. 05 Aug. 2016.

Allington, Richard L. *What Really Matters in Response to Intervention: Research-Based Designs*. Boston, MA: Pearson, 2009. Print.

Anderson, R. C., E. H. Hiebert, J. A. Scott, and I. A. Wilkinson. *Becoming a Nation of Readers: The Report of the Commission on Reading*. Washington, DC: National Institute of Education, 1985. Print.

Atwell, Nancie. *The Reading Zone: How to Help Kids Become Skilled, Passionate, Habitual, Critical Readers*. New York: Scholastic, 2007. Print.

Beers, G. Kylene, and Robert E. Probst. *Notice & Note: Strategies for Close Reading*. Portsmouth, NH: Heinemann, 2013. Print.

Bishop, Rudine Sims. "Mirrors, Windows, and Sliding Glass Doors." *Perspectives: Choosing and Using Books for the Learning Community* 6.3 (1990): n. pag. *Perspectives: Choosing and Using Books for the Learning Community*. Web. 12 June 2016.

Boardman, Alison Gould, Greg Roberts, Sharon Vaughn, Jade Wexler, Christy S. Murray, and Maria Kosanovich. "Effective Instruction for Adolescent Struggling Readers." *A Practice Brief* (2008): n. pag. Center for Instruction. Web. 30 Oct. 2016.

Cain, Susan. "The Power of Introverts." *The Huffington Post*. TheHuffingtonPost.com, 18 Apr. 2012. Web. 6 Nov. 2016.

Clark, Christina, Sarah Osborne, and George Dugdale. "Role Models and Young People's Reading." *Reaching Out With Role Models*. National Literacy Trust, Apr. 2009. Web. 7 Aug. 2016.

Collins, Fiona, Teresa Cremin, Marilyn Mottram, Sacha Powell, and Kimberly Safford. "Developing Teachers' Knowledge of Children's Literature: Teachers as Readers, Phase II." *Children's Books*. Books for Keeps, n.d. Web. 26 Aug. 2016.

Csikszentmihalyi, Mihaly. *Flow: The Psychology of Optimal Experience*. New York: Harper & Row, 1990. Print.

Davies, Matthew J. *Increasing Students' L2 Usage: An Analysis of Teacher Talk Time and Student Talk Time* (2011): n. pag. Dec. 2011. Web. 12 Mar. 2016.

Elley, Warwick B., and Francis Mangubhai. "The Long-Term Effects of a Book Flood on Children's Language Growth." *The Long-Term Effects of a Book Flood on Children's Language Growth* (n.d.): n. pag. *Directions: Journal of Educational Studies*. Institute of Educations, University of the South Pacific. Web. 12 Apr. 2016.

Fountas, Irene C. "Text Levels—Tool or Trouble?" *Lesley University Center for Reading Recovery and Literacy Collaborative*. n. pag., 23 Oct. 2013. Web. 06 Jan. 2016.

Fountas, Irene C., and Gay Su Pinnell. *Guided Reading: Good First Teaching for All Children*. Portsmouth, NH: Heinemann, 1996. Print.

Furrer, Carrie, and Ellen Skinner. "Sense of Relatedness as a Factor in Children's Academic Engagement and Performance." *Journal of Educational Psychology* 95.1 (2003): 148–162. Web.

Gallagher, Kelly. *Readicide How Schools Are Killing Reading and What You Can Do About It*. Portland, ME: Stenhouse, 2009. Print.

Gambrell, Linda. *Creating Learning Community Cultures That Foster Reading Motivation* (1996): n. pag. *Distinguished Educator Series*. International Reading Association, 1996. Web. 26 Oct. 2016.

Gambrell, Linda, and Barbara Marinak. "Reading Motivation: What the Research Says." *Reading Rockets*. n. pag., n.d. Web. 09 Sept. 2016.

Gelman, Lauren. "Benefits of Reading: Getting Smart, Thin, Healthy, Happy I Reader's Digest." *Readers Digest*. n. pag., n.d. Web. 06 Nov. 2016.

Heise, Jillian. "Celebrating a Culture of Literacy Displays." *Heise Reads & Recommends*. n. pag., 25 Mar. 2013. Web. 02 Apr. 2016.

Huck, Charlotte S., Susan Ingrid Hepler, and Janet Hickman. *Children's Literature in the Elementary School*. New York: Holt, Rinehart, and Winston, 1993. Print.

Irvin, Judith L., Julie Meltzer, and Melinda S. Dukes. *Taking Action on Adolescent Literacy: An Implementation Guide for School Leaders*. Alexandria, VA: Association for Supervision and Curriculum Development, 2007. Print.

Ivey, Gay, and Peter H. Johnston. "Engagement With Young Adult Literature: Outcomes and Processes." *Reading Research Quarterly* 48.3 (2013): 255–275. *Education Research Complete*. Web. 06 Jan. 2017.

Keene, Ellin Oliver, and Susan Zimmermann. *Mosaic of Thought: Teaching Comprehension in a Reader's Workshop*. Portsmouth, NH: Heinemann, 1997. Print.

Khazen, Olga. "Is Listening to Audio Books Really the Same as Reading?" *Forbes*. Forbes Magazine, 11 Sept. 2011. Web. 13 Apr. 2016.

"Kids and Family Reading Report." *Scholastic.com*. n. pag., 2014. Web. 09 Oct. 2016.

Kittle, Penny. *Book Love: Developing Depth, Stamina, and Passion in Adolescent Readers*. Portsmouth, NH: Heinemann, 2013. Print.

Krashen, Stephen. *Free Voluntary Reading: New Research, Applications, and Controversies* (2004): n. pag. Apr. 2004. Web. Oct. 2016.

Krashen, Stephen. "Sustained Silent Reading: The Effects Are Substantial, It Works, and It Leads to More Reading. A Response to Shanahan (2016)." *SKrashen*. n. pag., 09 Oct. 2016. Web. 09 Oct. 2016.

Krashen, Stephen. *The Power of Reading Insights from the Research*. Westport, CT: Libraries Unlimited, 2004. Print.

Lesesne, Teri S. *Reading Ladders: Leading Students From Where They Are to Where We'd Like Them to Be*. Portsmouth, NH: Heinemann, 2010. Print.

Lin, Qiuyun. "Parent Involvement and Early Literacy/Browse Our Publications/Publications & Resources/HFRP—Harvard Family Research Project." *Parent Involvement and Early Literacy/Browse Our Publications/Publications & Resources/HFRP—Harvard Family Research Project*. Harvard Family Research Project, Oct. 2003. Web. 06 Nov. 2016.

Miller, Donalyn. *The Book Whisperer: Awakening the Inner Reader in Every Child*. San Francisco, CA: Jossey-Bass, 2009. Print.

Miller, Donalyn, and Susan Kelley. *Reading in the Wild: The Book Whisperer's Keys to Cultivating Lifelong Reading Habits*. San Francisco, CA: Jossey-Bass, 2013. Print.

Murray, Robert, and Catherine Ramstetter. "The Crucial Role of Recess in School." *American Academy of Pediatrics Policy Statement* 131.1 (2013): n. pag. *Table of Contents*. Council on School Health, Jan. 2013. Web. 07 Oct. 2016.

Nadworny, Elissa. "Middle School Suicides Reach an All-Time High." *NPR*. NPR, 04 Nov. 2016. Web. 7 Nov. 2016.

"NAEP—2015 Mathematics & Reading Assessments." *NAEP—2015 Mathematics & Reading Assessments*. n. pag., n.d. Web. 06 Nov. 2016.

National Endowment for the Arts. Reading at Risk: A Survey of Reading in America. Washington D.C., n.d. PDF.

Neuman, Susan B. "Reading Literature on Screen in a Classroom Library." *The Importance of the Classroom Library* (1999): n. pag. Scholastic. Web. 16 May 2016.

Newkirk, Thomas. "Reading Is Not a Race: The Virtues of the 'Slow Reading' Movement." *The Washington Post*. n. pag., 30 Jan. 2012. Web. 13 Feb. 2016.

Newkirk, Thomas. *The Art of Slow Reading: Six Time-Honored Practices for Engagement*. Portsmouth, NH: Heinemann, 2012. Print.

Parrish, Mary. "Goal Setting and Reading Achievement." *Abstract* (n.d.): n. pag. 6 July 2014. Web. 16 July 2016.

Perrin, Andrew. "Social Media Usage: 2005–2015." *Pew Research Center Internet Science Tech RSS*. n. pag., 08 Oct. 2015. Web. 09 Nov. 2016.

Rainie, Lee, and Andrew Perrin. "Slightly Fewer Americans Are Reading Print Books, New Survey Finds." *Pew Research Center RSS*. n. pag., 19 Oct. 2015. Web. 06 Nov. 2016.

Ripp, Pernille. *Passionate Learners: How to Engage and Empower Your Students*. 2nd ed. New York: Routledge, 2016. Print.

Routman, Regie. *Reading Essentials: The Specifics You Need to Teach Reading Well*. Portsmouth, NH: Heinemann, 2003. Print.

Serravallo, Jennifer. *The Reading Strategies Book: Your Everything Guide to Developing Skilled Readers*. Portsmouth, NH: Heinemann, 2015. Print.

Shabazz, Ilyasah. Malcolm Little: The Little Boy Who became Malcolm X. New York, NY: Atheneum Books for Young Readers, 2014. Print.

Short, Kathy Gnagey, and Kathryn Mitchell Pierce. *Talking About Books: Creating Literate Communities*. Portsmouth, NH: Heinemann, 1990. Print.

"Social Media Use Among College Students and Teens: What's In, What's Out, and Why." *Modo Labs*. n. pag., 26 Apr. 2016. Web. 09 Nov. 2016.

Spiegel, Dixie Lee. "Silver Bullets, Babies, and Bath Water: Literature Response Groups in a Balanced Literacy Program." *The Reading Teacher* 52.2 (1998): 114–124. Web. 02 Nov. 2016.

"Statement on Classroom Libraries." *National Council of Teachers of English*. NCTE, May 2017. Web. 06 June 2017. <http://www.ncte.org/positions/statements/classroom-libraries>.

Stauffer, Russell G. "Reading as Experience in Inquiry." (1967): n. pag. Association for Supervision and Curriculum Development. Web. 01 Nov. 2016.

Willingham, Daniel. "Is Listening to an Audio Book 'Cheating?'" *Daniel Willingham*. N.pag., 24 July 2016. Web. 13 Nov. 2016.

Wong, Harry K., and Rosemary T. Wong. "Learning Community Management 2: Consistency Is Key | Scholastic.com." *Scholastic Teachers*. n. pag., n.d. Web. 06 Sept. 2016.